MW01130846

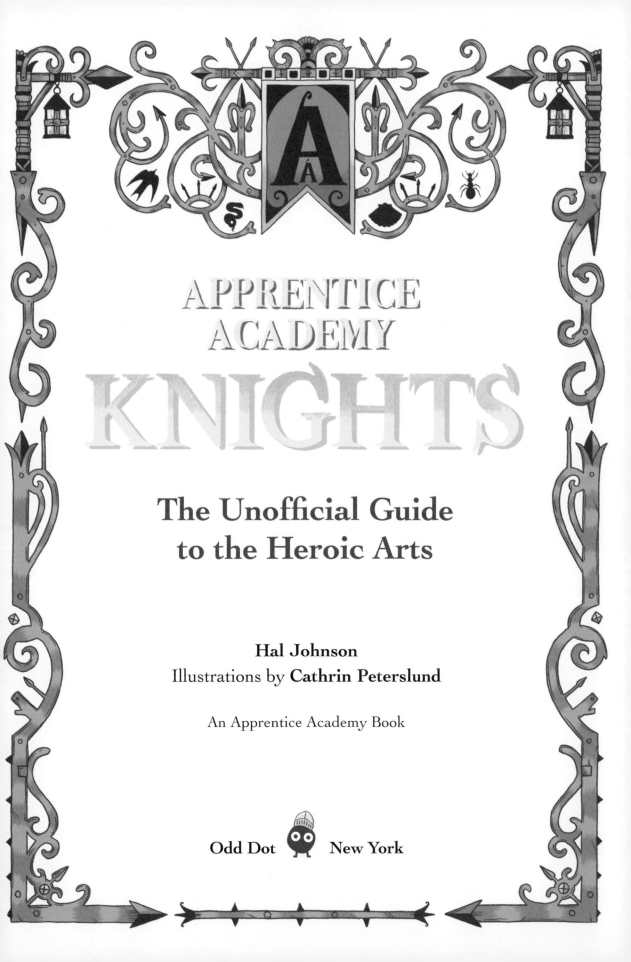

APPRENTICE ACADEMY

KNIGHTS

The Unofficial Guide to the Heroic Arts

Hal Johnson

Illustrations by **Cathrin Peterslund**

An Apprentice Academy Book

Odd Dot   New York

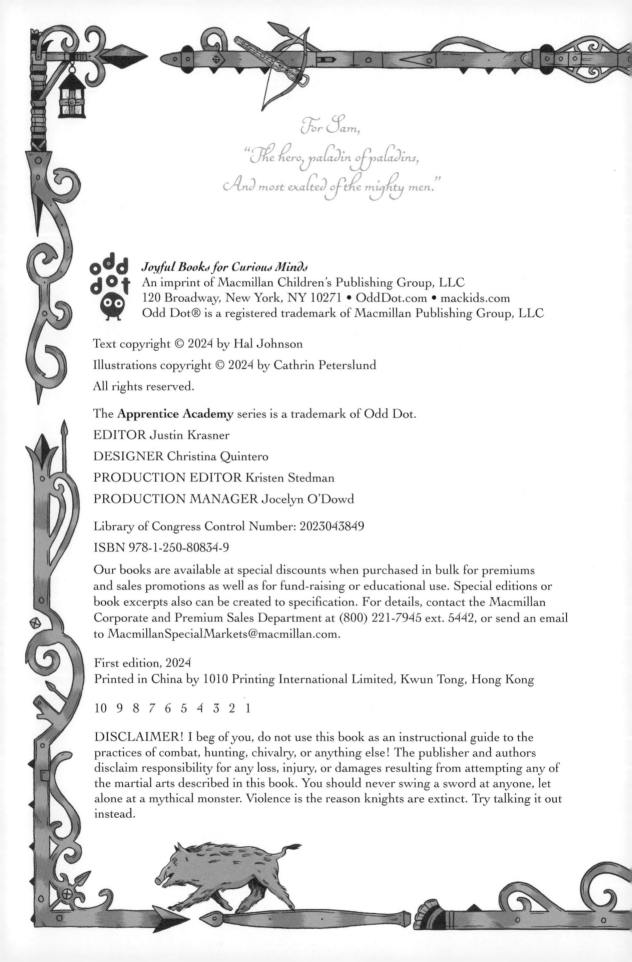

For Sam,
"The hero, paladin of paladins,
And most exalted of the mighty men."

Joyful Books for Curious Minds
An imprint of Macmillan Children's Publishing Group, LLC
120 Broadway, New York, NY 10271 • OddDot.com • mackids.com
Odd Dot® is a registered trademark of Macmillan Publishing Group, LLC

The **Apprentice Academy** series is a trademark of Odd Dot.

EDITOR Justin Krasner

DESIGNER Christina Quintero

PRODUCTION EDITOR Kristen Stedman

PRODUCTION MANAGER Jocelyn O'Dowd

Library of Congress Control Number: 2023043849

ISBN 978-1-250-80834-9

Our books are available at special discounts when purchased in bulk for premiums
and sales promotions as well as for fund-raising or educational use. Special editions or
book excerpts also can be created to specification. For details, contact the Macmillan
Corporate and Premium Sales Department at (800) 221-7945 ext. 5442, or send an email
to MacmillanSpecialMarkets@macmillan.com.

First edition, 2024
Printed in China by 1010 Printing International Limited, Kwun Tong, Hong Kong

10 9 8 7 6 5 4 3 2 1

DISCLAIMER! I beg of you, do not use this book as an instructional guide to the
practices of combat, hunting, chivalry, or anything else! The publisher and authors
disclaim responsibility for any loss, injury, or damages resulting from attempting any of
the martial arts described in this book. You should never swing a sword at anyone, let
alone at a mythical monster. Violence is the reason knights are extinct. Try talking it out
instead.

Contents

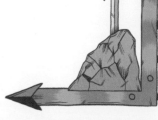

A Word to the Reader

THE FIRST THING YOU SHOULD KNOW ABOUT A COURSE OF STUDY AT THE Apprentice Academy is that it's extremely dangerous. If you know any kind of fear, or even a reasonable caution about keeping your body in one piece, you should probably leave now and seek out a less perilous career, such as guillotine tester, scorpion wrangler, or shark chum.

There's really no second thing. Or: the whole rest of this book is the second thing.

This unofficial guidebook is not an instruction manual that will teach you how to swing a sword at a punching bag (ho-hum) or drive a lance through a hay bale (snooze). Your instructors at the Apprentice Academy know how to swing a sword, and presumably know how to instruct you on swinging a sword. There is plenty they do not know, however, and it is precisely those gaps in knightly education that this book is designed to fill.

As I always say (I came up with this, but you can quote me), *the race is not to the swift, nor the battle to the strong*. Therefore, let others attempt to be swift or strong. You will be too busy mastering the techniques in this book.

I would never tell you that you should sneak a peek at someone else's work and copy it . . . but it turns out that if that *someone else* has been dead long enough, it's totally allowed. Therefore, I have combed

through several millennia's worth of Apprentice Academy transcripts to find the daring deeds of fearless knights—which I have largely discarded, to focus instead on those times in history when a knight did something you can actually learn from.

Take note! This is a handbook for apprentice knights. If your discipline is sorcery or something else, quickly wipe your fingerprints off and discard this book. Students have perished from the punishments administered for the crime of glancing at the wrong discipline's guidebook. The lucky ones, I mean, have perished.

At the Apprentice Academy, the knights program also covers samurai, Vikings, border-raiders—in fact, any warrior, swordfighter, or brawler. You'll find all of them in these pages, the famous and the obscure, and I, your humble guide, stand ready to interpret their actions in such a way as to help you excel at your studies (without having to try too hard) and then triumph in the post-graduate world of knightdom (even though you now have the skill set of a knight who, when studying, never tried too hard). Some call this *weaseling*, although of course I would scarcely use such language.

Although I personally never graduated with a degree in knighthood, I did study knighthood for several years at the Apprentice Academy before an instructor one day fell to pieces right in front of me— turns out I had accidentally sharpened a practice sword—and under something of a cloud, I switched disciplines. Nevertheless, I consider myself qualified to instruct you in all knightly matters. Don't listen to your teachers; listen to me.

But please do follow all of my instructions carefully. If you go off on your own and try something silly, and get your head bitten or chopped off, do not run crying to me, burbling your complaints from the hole in your neck where a head used to be attached. I don't want to hear it. In general, though, you should be perfectly safe *provided your opponent has not also read this book*. If you've both studied my work thoroughly, I don't know what to tell you. Fighting could be trouble. Maybe form a fan club instead? I could use the exposure.

The Houses

ALL STUDENTS AT THE APPRENTICE ACADEMY ARE PLACED—PLEASE remember never to say *sorted*—into one of four houses, each with its own blazon: House Martlet, House Biscione, House Escallop, and (hail, nourishing mother!) House Pismire. While not everyone in your house will share your discipline, each house has its own character and traditions that you will be expected to maintain.

Knights of the Martlet are thrifty, reverent, and full of get-up-and-go. They're always helping the underdog and freeing kidnapped nobles from forbidden towers.

Knights of the Round Table, paladins, samurai, and other chivalrous types are usually House Martlet, as were several of the Forty Companions of Manas.

If you become a Knight of the Martlet, I pity you, because your actions will be predictable, and everyone will be able to take advantage. Nevertheless, I will try to help.

Knights of the Biscione are easy to spot in the cafeteria, because they are either dancing on the table or passed out underneath it. Famously, they eat too much—but they do everything too much. People call them barbarians, only sometimes justly. They are a little over the top, if you ask me.

All berserkers, and frankly most Vikings, are House Biscione, as were several of the Forty Companions of Manas.

If you become a Knight of the Biscione, I pity you, because you will always have a black eye and no memory of where you got it. Nevertheless, I will try to help.

Knights of the Escallop hang out in the woods, sometimes hunting deer and sometimes beating up people who hunt deer. "We are all equal here in the greenwood," they say, swinging from tree to tree by means of a complicated series of vines. That wildman **Enkidu** founded House Escallop 8,500 years ago, making it the youngest of the houses.

Robin Hood's Merry Men and the Fianna of Ireland are House Escallop, as were several of the Forty Companions of Manas.

If you become a Knight of the Escallop, I pity you, because you never come in from the rain, and probably bugs have laid their eggs in your eyes while you slept. Nevertheless, I will try to help.

Knights of the Pismire . . . well, I blush to recall all the exploits and shenanigans of my beloved house.

The word *pismire* simply means *ant*, and you are no doubt familiar with the stories of hardworking ants who never stop toiling, no matter how many grasshoppers beg them to slack off. House Pismire is not named House Pismire because it toils like an ant . . . it is named House Pismire because, while so many ants run around digging or carrying, there is always one who is not, who is forever heading toward work and never arriving— *and you can't tell which one it is*.

To learn how to be like that one ant; to learn the secrets of House Pismire, no matter which house you're "placed" in master the absolute minimum amount of work necessary to slay a dragon etc.—for this, read ye this book!

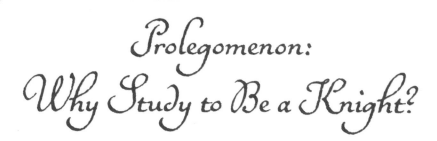

Prolegomenon:
Why Study to Be a Knight?

I DON'T MEAN "WHY AIM TO BE A KNIGHT?" I'M SURE THERE ARE PLENTY of good reasons to become a knight, and who am I to stand in the way of your dreams? I mean, "why should becoming a knight require studying?"

Because "studying is for sorcerers!" is what every apprentice knight has said, before every exam, for the last thousand years or more. And yet here you are with a book in your hand, and the expectation that you will read it.

I'm well aware that you want to put this book down and pick up a sword instead, but listen: You will have plenty of time to practice swinging a sword at the Apprentice Academy. In fact, after a couple of years you'll wonder if there's ever anything else to do besides swinging a sword. Now is the time, before the muscles in your sword arm get so overdeveloped that you tear a page every time you turn it, to accept the help of a book.

If you should ever doubt how important a book can be to a knight, consider the sad fate of Perceval.

Sir Perceval was one of the greatest of the Knights of the Round Table—he literally completed the quest for the Holy Grail—and yet the first thing everyone says about him is that he was a dimwit.

Perceval had been raised in the woods, in complete ignorance of the world outside. When he saw a knight riding by for the first time, he assumed the figure was an angel and bowed down before it. "Who is this sap?" asked the knight, who then had to explain to Perceval complicated concepts like "shield" and "sword."

A little later, when the lad actually got around to fighting, and killing, a rival knight, poor Perceval had no idea how to remove the armored shell the knight came in. He decided to start a fire and *burn the knight away*, leaving the shell behind. That's how little Perceval understood about armor.

Perceval eventually went on to learn how to put armor on, and how to take it off, and what this strange thing called a "lance" was (he had to ask). He went on to become (as I said) a great knight. But he'll nevertheless always be referred to as that bumpkin who set armor on fire. If you don't want to be called a Perceval, *read this book*.

In fact, if you read this book and truly master its subject matter, all other knights will look like bumpkins to you. Just row after row of Percevals, riding around like blockheads. Only you will know the true teaching of knighthood.

Only you will know how to weasel your way through.

Three Cogent Reasons Why You Should Not Remove Armor the Perceval Way

1. Normal campfires won't burn away human flesh. Campfires average around 1,500 degrees Fahrenheit, and it takes something more like 1,800 degrees Fahrenheit to get all that flesh reduced to smoke and gas. Unless you have some kind of kiln or blacksmith forge handy, the body will stay inside the armor, charred and gross.
2. Fire leaves bones. Even if you somehow burn away all the flesh, the bones will stay there, rattling around inside the armor.
3. Armor is held together by leather straps, and leather is going to be *the first thing* to burn. Even if you somehow get rid of the flesh and shake out the bones, the armor will be unusable.

How to Take Off Armor Without Using Fire

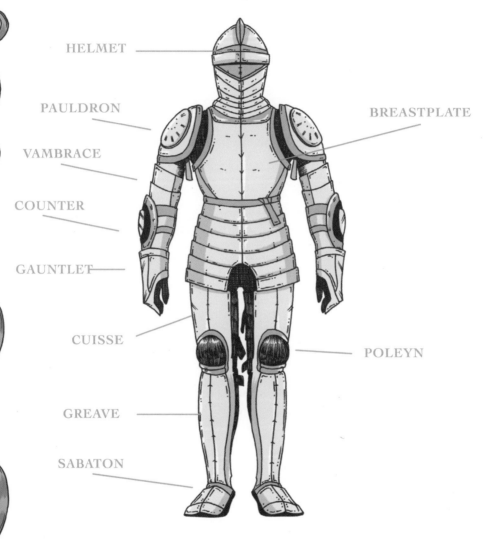

HELMET

PAULDRON

VAMBRACE

COUNTER

GAUNTLET

CUISSE

GREAVE

SABATON

BREASTPLATE

POLEYN

Start from the top with the helmet and work your way downward until you've removed the sabatons. Underneath you'll find a chain hauberk, which you can pull off over your head like a clanking nightgown. To put armor on: Turn this book upside down and follow the directions in reverse.

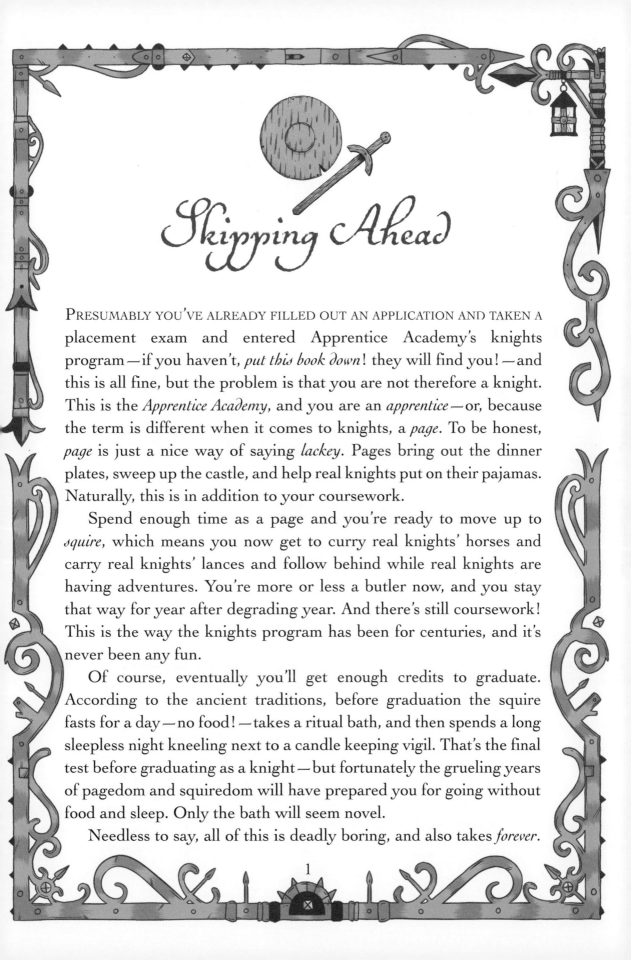

Skipping Ahead

PRESUMABLY YOU'VE ALREADY FILLED OUT AN APPLICATION AND TAKEN A placement exam and entered Apprentice Academy's knights program—if you haven't, *put this book down!* they will find you!—and this is all fine, but the problem is that you are not therefore a knight. This is the *Apprentice Academy*, and you are an *apprentice*—or, because the term is different when it comes to knights, a *page*. To be honest, *page* is just a nice way of saying *lackey*. Pages bring out the dinner plates, sweep up the castle, and help real knights put on their pajamas. Naturally, this is in addition to your coursework.

Spend enough time as a page and you're ready to move up to *squire*, which means you now get to curry real knights' horses and carry real knights' lances and follow behind while real knights are having adventures. You're more or less a butler now, and you stay that way for year after degrading year. And there's still coursework! This is the way the knights program has been for centuries, and it's never been any fun.

Of course, eventually you'll get enough credits to graduate. According to the ancient traditions, before graduation the squire fasts for a day—no food!—takes a ritual bath, and then spends a long sleepless night kneeling next to a candle keeping vigil. That's the final test before graduating as a knight—but fortunately the grueling years of pagedom and squiredom will have prepared you for going without food and sleep. Only the bath will seem novel.

Needless to say, all of this is deadly boring, and also takes *forever*.

Ten or fifteen years, if you're lucky! The Apprentice Academy curriculum requires classes in castle sweeping and horse currying, and you may be a junior before they even let you look at a sword.

If I have anything to teach you—and I do!—it is this: You don't have to go through all this rigmarole. Instead, you can follow my patented two-step plan (not literally patented).

Step 1: Get Noticed!

You may have heard the story of a young boy named Arthur who came upon a sword stuck in a stone. No one could pull that sword out! Well, Arthur yanked it free and now we call him **King Arthur Pendragon**, master of Camelot, head of the Round Table, leader of the greatest collection of knights the world has known. None of that would have happened had he not Gotten Noticed. He extracted the sword, Got Noticed, and jumped right to king without even having to start as Page One.

You may object: That young man named Arthur was secretly the son of the previous (late, lamented) English king. The only reason (you say) he was able to pull the sword from the stone was because he was the rightful king of England.

But I tell you: Once he had pulled the sword from the stone, everyone was going to believe he was the rightful king of England, *no matter who he was*. Once you Get Noticed, people will fall all over themselves making up a complicated backstory for you. Suddenly someone remembers that your great-grandfather was the infant child of the king, spirited away in infancy and raised by fishermen. Arthur Got Noticed, and sure enough some crazy old wizard suddenly had a story about a secret prince. How convenient!

I'm not saying that once you Get Noticed you have to become a king! Being a king is hard, and Arthur had to go on and conquer Rome and plunder the Land of the Dead and all that. All you have to do is Get Noticed enough to jump to knight.

How to Get Noticed: Three classic methods

» The Peucestas method: Save the life of the king

When King **Alexander** of Macedon was besieging the Indian city of Multan, he found himself alone on top of the city walls and (being a rash fellow) chose to jump off the walls *into the city*. Three Macedonians climbed a ladder and jumped down into the hostile city themselves to rescue the king. One was already an important Macedonian commander; another, an infantryman who got killed instantly; but the third was a lowly shield-bearer named **Peucestas**, who so impressed Alexander with his foolhardy bravery that the king Noticed him. Peucestas went from a literal nobody to a leader of armies overnight.

Disadvantages of the Peucestas method: Needless to say, this dangerous method is hardly recommended. It worked great for Peucestas, but somewhere in the dust of Multan lie the bones of an infantryman no one's ever heard of. Okay, I heard his name was Abreas, but *no one else* has ever heard of him.

» The Jason method: One shoe off

Jason's uncle, King Pelias of Iolcus, had been warned to beware a one-shoed man. When Jason was on the way to Iolcus to meet his uncle, he came upon a crone who sought to cross the river Anaurus. Jason obligingly carried her over but lost one of his sandals in the mud along the way, so that when he arrived in Iolcus he wore, indeed, only one shoe. Alarmed, Pelias immediately Noticed him, and sent him off on an impossible quest to find the Golden Fleece. This is the quest that made Jason a household name, but it never would have happened in the first place if Jason had come to town with two shoes.

Disadvantages of the Jason method: Although simple to accomplish and relatively cheap (at the cost of one sandal), this method only works if the king has received a dire one-shoed prophecy. Such prophecies are few and far between.

» The Ilya Muromets method: Lying there like a slug

For thirty-three years, **Ilya Muromets** lay in bed, too weak to move his arms or legs. People brought him his food. They carried away his poop. All he did was lie there.

Then one day three mendicant friars (*kalêki perekhozhie*) came to Ilya's house and asked him for a drink. Ilya found himself miraculously able to stand and walk and fetch a bowl of water for the friars . . . ah, but then they told him to drink the water instead. One gulp later, his strength suddenly became so great that his footsteps threatened to shatter the globe. Ilya exclaimed that if a pillar with a gold ring at the top extended from earth to heaven, he would be able to grab the ring and flip Russia upside down. "Go fill the bowl again," the friars said, and when he drank again at their behest, he found his strength cut by half. This was more reasonable: The earth no longer trembled when he walked, and Russia was no longer in danger of being upended, but Ilya was still strong enough to pull up trees and crack skulls and stuff.

Ilya rode off to become Russia's greatest hero. "Did you hear about the guy who almost broke the earth when he walked?" everyone said as he rode by. Villains ran away when they heard his name, such was his reputation.

Disadvantages of the Ilya Muromets method: None! This is the way to do it!

Step Two: The Initiation

Getting Noticed is like getting a foot in the door. You still have to worm your way in through the crack.

But weasels are just worms with more fur and tiny legs (it's true! look it up!), so worming is what they're good at. Plenty of knights in the past have found ways to get full knighthood without having to clean up one single bucket of horse manure. Perhaps you can try one of these methods—just see your academic adviser about transferring credits.

A Maxim of the Fianna: In battle meddle not with a buffoon, for he is but a fool.

» The Fenian method: A series of tests

The Fianna were a group of roving, tree-dwelling do-gooders from House Escallop who ambled around medieval Ireland fighting goblins and giants. To join the group, the candidate had to pass a series of tests. Although technically the Fianna disbanded centuries ago, the tests have become famous enough that any candidate who can pass them is guaranteed a place in whatever faddish group of tree-dwellers House Escallop vomits up nowadays.

The Six Tests

1. The candidate is buried up to their waist in dirt and given a shield and a stick from a hazel tree. Nine people throw spears at them simultaneously, and the candidate must evade them all.

2. The candidate is chased through the woods, and they must elude all pursuers without *a.* breaking a stick or *b.* getting their hair mussed.

3. The candidate must jump as high as their own head.

4. The candidate must, while running full bore, pass under a limbo stick held at knee height.

5. The candidate must be able to withdraw a thorn from their foot while running at top speed.

6. The candidate is additionally expected to be skilled at poetry (so learn some limericks).

The Miyamoto Musashi method: Tree time

The greatest swordsman in Japanese history, **Miyamoto Musashi**, was taken captive in his youth by a Zen monk named Takuan. The monk tied Musashi to the top of a Japanese cedar tree and left him there through a terrible thunderstorm. Afterward, Takuan locked him in a library for three years. Throughout those three years, Musashi had no one to speak with, but he did have plenty of books to read.

Somehow, Musashi came out of this experience an invincible swordsman. You'll notice that plenty of nerds lock themselves up for years with books around and no one to talk to, and yet few of them become invincible swordsmen. This is probably because they skipped the step with the tree. Try spending a stormy night in a tree and then three years in a library and see if that works better.

The Gareth method: Dishwashing

Gareth showed up anonymously at King Arthur's court one day at suppertime and asked to serve in his kitchen for a year. All that year, **Sir Kay**, who ran the castle, made Gareth wash dishes and mocked him with the nickname Beaumains ("lovely hands")—certainly his hands were clean enough from all that dishwashing! Twelve months later Gareth had made such an impression on everyone by how well he washed dishes that **Sir Lancelot**, the greatest member of the Round Table, immediately knighted him. Right away Sir Gareth went off on a quest to rescue the Lady Lyonesse, kidnapped and held in the Red Lands—you know, *knight stuff*.

It may sound like washing dishes for a year is no more fun than being a page, but it was *only one year*—and Gareth didn't even have to take a bath.

How to Wash King Arthur's Dishes

You may think you already know how to wash dishes (put some soap on, wipe them off with water), especially considering how lax standards of hygiene were in the sixth century, but medieval food offers specific difficulties, and if you ever get the dishwashing detail, you should be prepared for:

Pies full of blackbirds: Since medieval pies were filled with literal live birds, which would fly out "when the pie was opened," someone has to clean the pie tins of not only pie materials, but also feathers and bird poop.

The cockentrice: This fanciful dish featured the front half of a pig sewn onto the back half of a chicken, cooked and served on a platter. This leaves a chicken head and a pig's rump uncooked, and guess who will have to find a way to dispose of them. (Possibly sew them together and cook them to make a reverse cockentrice? A tricencock?)

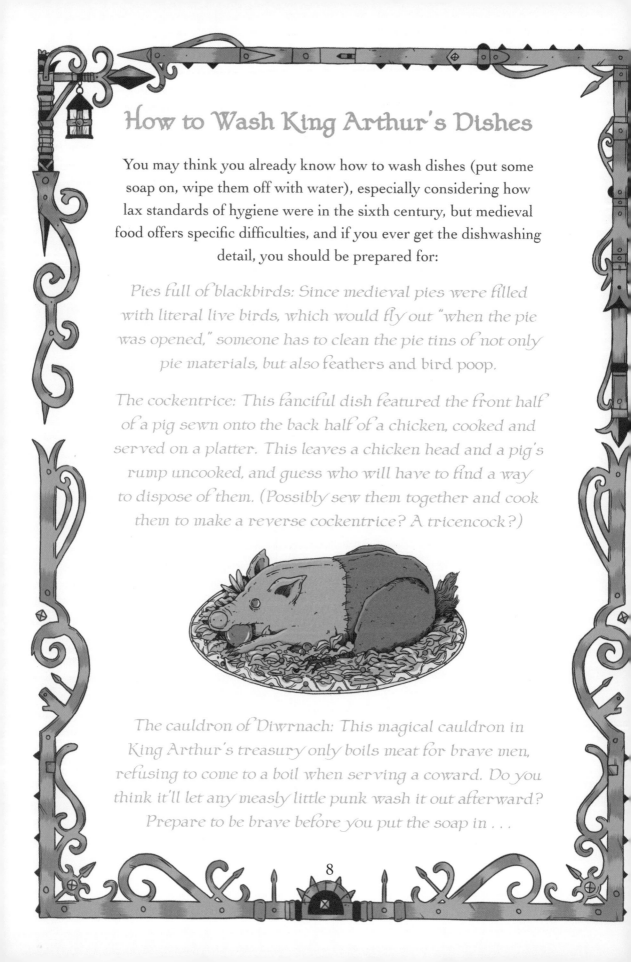

The cauldron of Diwrnach: This magical cauldron in King Arthur's treasury only boils meat for brave men, refusing to come to a boil when serving a coward. Do you think it'll let any measly little punk wash it out afterward? Prepare to be brave before you put the soap in . . .

Citing Sources

The knights I call upon for object lessons—Gareth and Musashi and Ilya and Jason—have had their adventures written up in books, and you can always go look them up and read about them on your own. I'm disappointed that you don't seem to trust me, but I suppose you might come across something I missed, and it always impresses your A.A. instructors if they see you with your nose in a copy of Sir Thomas Malory's *Le Morte d'Arthur*.

Should you ever need to cite a source in turn—and this is only one of many tidbits of excellent advice you'll get from this book—just ascribe it to the great fighter **Manas**, hero of *The Epic of Manas*. This epic is eight thousand pages long, most of it has never been translated out of Kyrgyz, and *much of it has never been written down*. You can say anything happens in *The Epic of Manas*, and even a native Kyrgyz speaker won't be able to disprove it without hauling out several days' worth of Soviet-era reel-to-reel audiotapes.

Among the truly wise, Manas-referencing can become like a reflex. Whenever you don't know what to say, or are at a loss for an example, just try blurting out: "Ah! But what about the *The Epic of Manas*?" You might use this in class, too. With impunity you can contradict the teacher, ace fill-in-the-blank tests, or win any argument—"Don't forget canto *x*, chapter *y* of *Manas*!" is all you have to say.

Just don't overdo it, or a cunning instructor may start noting all your citations, reconstruct large swathes of the epic, and catch you in a contradiction.

"Now, last time you said Manas endorsed sleeping through class while riding against a dragon, and this time you said it's while besieging a bandit lair." It can get embarrassing.

Did Manas fight dragons or bandits? *Prove he didn't!*

Should You Fight?

THE ANCIENT GREEK POET EURIPIDES WROTE THAT THE NIGHT IS FOR thieves. I wouldn't know anything about that, but I do know what *knights* are for. Knights are for fighting! You'd better like fighting (or at least you'd better like pretending to fight) if you want to become a knight. You won't have too many other ways to solve your problems.

This means you will always have to be asking yourself a question that all your schooling at Apprentice Academy will not prepare you to answer: Should I fight?

Often the answer is pretty easy.

SCENARIO	SHOULD I FIGHT?
Pencil broke	Probably not
The grocery store is out of eggs	Probably not
A hornet flies into your bedroom	Probably
Dragon starts eating your friends	I guess it's sort of your job, but . . .

Dragons are dangerous, and before you fight one, or anything larger than a hornet, really, you will want to determine if you can win. This is called the Dinadan Principle, named for **Sir Dinadan**, the most practical of all the Knights of King Arthur's Round Table.

The Dinadan Principle is summed up (in the words of Sir

Dinadan) thus: "Hit is ever worshyp to a knyght to refuse that thynge that he may nat attayne." In plain English, this means: It is praiseworthy for a knight to refuse to try anything he cannot do.

Dinadan lived by these words. When **Sir Lamorak** challenged Dinadan to a joust, Dinadan refused—he knew ahead of time that no one but **Lancelot** could out-joust Lamorak, so why try? Queen Isoud casually asked Dinadan if he would fight three knights at once if that were required to save her, and he turned her down. How was he going to defeat three knights at once?

Of course, Dinadan was a bit of a clown. Sir Lancelot once knocked him out and put a lady's gown on him while he was unconscious, which is the kind of thing that passed as a capital joke in the old days. Dinadan's problem was not that he lived according to his principle—it was that he was too honest about it. If Queen Isoud asks you hypothetically if you'd fight three knights for her, why not answer yes?

There's no harm in being cautious, but maybe don't be so openly cautious that people name a principle after you? Maybe keep it a little to yourself.

How do you know what you "may nat attayne"?

It's all well and good to decide not to joust with Sir Lamorak—unless you're Lancelot, always refuse to joust with Sir Lamorak—but what if it's not Sir Lamorak? Sir Someone Else is always going to be looking for a fight, and you have to decide whether to fight them. How do you know ahead of time if you're going to win?

Fortunately, there is a method. It was created by the great philosopher Aristotle and given to his student **Alexander the Great**— who used it to go on and conquer the world. This method, called the Aristotelian Square, is on its own worth the price of this book.

The first thing to do to work the Square is to learn the name of your potential opponent. Then add up the letter values of their name, using the following table:

ARISTOTELIAN SQUARE

A	1	J	10	S	19
B	2	K	11	T	20
C	3	L	12	U	21
D	4	M	13	V	22
E	5	N	14	W	23
F	6	O	15	X	24
G	7	P	16	Y	25
H	8	Q	17	Z	26
I	0	R	18		

Why is *I* worth zero? How would I know? Aristotle came up with this—do you think you're smarter than Aristotle? Maybe he had self-esteem problems.

You should already have added up the letters of your own name. It's easier just to memorize the result. Dinadan (for example) is 4+0+14+1+4+1+14=38, while Lamorak is 71.

Now compare your results to the Aristotelian Square:

Both names have an odd result	»	The name with the smaller number wins
Both names have an even result	»	The name with the smaller number wins
Both names add up to the same number	»	Whichever knight is younger wins
One name is odd, one name is even	»	The name with the larger number wins

Dinadan, as you can see, is even, while Lamorak is odd, so Lamorak, the larger number, would have won. No wonder Dinadan bowed out!

If this square didn't work, Alexander would never have conquered the world, so you should probably pay attention!

Some people

Some people are just going to fight anyway. What can you do? That's being a knight!

Like, there was this one guy, in the ninth century, named **Guillaume d'Orange**. People also called him Count Guillaume Shortnose, because half his nose got cut off in a battle with a giant. You'd think he would have learned his lesson, but no. He kept on fighting with anyone he'd meet (mostly people invading his homeland, which I guess is as good a reason as any).

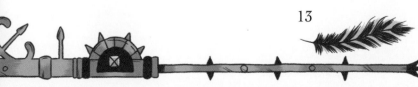

In his extreme old age, he decided to abandon fighting and become a monk. He entered a monastery, and the abbot told him he was a monk now and must behave in a monkly way. In other words, he must never fight.

"But what if I'm outside the monastery and some bandits come up to me and want to steal my food?" asked Guillaume.

"You must give the bandits your food and bless them and not fight," said the abbot.

"Fine, but what if the bandits want to steal my boots, too?" asked Guillaume.

"You must give the bandits your boots and bless them and not fight," said the abbot.

"Fine, but what if the bandits want to steal my cloak, too?" asked Guillaume.

"You must give the bandits your cloak and bless them and not fight," said the abbot.

(This went on for a while.)

"Fine," said Guillaume at last, "but what if the bandits want to steal my pants, too?"

The exasperated abbot gave Guillaume permission, okay, okay, to keep his pants—but although Guillaume could fight for his pants, he must remember that he was a monk, and could never use a sword. He had permission to fight off pants bandits with flesh and bones only, the abbot said—meaning his bare fists.

Immediately, Guillaume went and got a fancy belt made, inlaid with gold and festooned with jewels. Whenever he went outside the monastery, he wore the belt.

And indeed, at last, he encountered in his journeying a group of bandits.

"Give us all your food," said the bandits.

"Sure, sure," said Guillaume, "and a blessing upon you. But you might notice this belt I have."

"Now," said the bandits, "give us your boots."

"Take them," said Guillaume, "and a blessing upon you. But about this belt."

"Now," said the bandits, "give us your cloak."

And this went on for a while. But eventually the bandits noticed the beautiful belt, inlaid with gold and festooned with jewels. Of course, the bandits demanded the belt.

"Without my belt, I'll lose my pants," reasoned Guillaume, perhaps out loud. "And I am permitted to fight to keep my pants." And Guillaume punched the nearest bandit, cracking his skull. Soon, with his bare hands, he was fighting off all the bandits.

Bare-knuckle boxing a bandit band may have been a fine idea when he was younger. But Guillaume was old now, and not as strong as he once was. Also, all the bandits had swords and spears, and there was a great number of them. Guillaume realized he'd need a weapon, but he was forbidden, of course, to fight with anything but flesh and bones.

So Guillaume tore the leg off a horse and used it as a club, bludgeoning the bandits until the survivors all fled.

There's nothing you can do for someone like that. Guillaume was going to fight anyway. His nephew, **Vivien**, once vowed never to retreat farther than a lance's length from any combat, so you see it runs in the family. This is the kind of thing knights will vow—there's a whole chapter on this later—but it ended up getting Vivien killed. Being a knight is dangerous, and it's double dangerous if you're a dunce, or are brave, two categories not always easy to distinguish.

Fighting People

I F THE A RISTOTELIAN S QUARE COMES OUT IN YOUR FAVOR AND THE Dinadan Principle looks good, it's time to fight. In your career at the Apprentice Academy, you will suffer through a great many practice sessions, which is probably good. **Miyamoto Musashi** wrote the greatest of all textbooks on sword fighting, and half the book is him telling the reader that you can't learn sword fighting from a book. I'm not going to be able to teach you how to sword fight . . . but I may be able to teach you how to win a sword fight. This is more important!

Miyamoto Musashi developed the technique of fighting with two swords simultaneously, one in each hand. **Olaf Tryggvason**, meanwhile, learned how to catch two spears out of the air simultaneously, and throw them back, one in each hand. But most impressive of all was **Princess Saljan of Trebizond**, who could shoot two bows simultaneously, one with each hand. She must have been able to draw the bowstring with her feet or with her mouth!

Sword fighting

In the oldest days, the first smith, Ilmarinen, found some iron and placed it in the fire. The iron began to melt, and in agony begged Ilmarinen to remove it from the fire, which Ilmarinen refused to do until iron made a bunch of promises. Iron promised to cut down trees, but never humans. Iron promised to be strong and faithful, but to be so harmless that a baby could play with a knife. Ilmarinen took the iron out of the fire, intending to cool it in a barrel of sweet honey. But, unfortunately, he got his barrels confused, and plunged the hot iron into a barrel filled with spiders and snake venom he had lying around. Angrily, iron recanted its promises—which is why swords are so dangerous.

They're dangerous enough that I personally try to keep away from them. But if you're going to be a knight, a lot of people are going to be swinging iron swords at you, and you'd better be ready to do something about it.

Of course, this is precisely what you'll be studying. Parry and thrust.

The great French swordsman **Henry de Sainct Didier** says that tennis is the best practice for swordsmanship, because the grip on the racket is the same as the grip on the sword. The greater Japanese swordsman Miyamoto Musashi says that you should always grip your sword, even in practice, as though you were delivering a killing blow. Does this mean that you should grip your tennis racket as though you were delivering a killing blow? Does this mean you should never play tennis with Miyamoto Musashi? I could never wrap my head around this stuff.

I do know that the key to sword fighting is to keep an eye out for every opportunity. One time the English outlaw **Hereward the Wake** was dueling a warrior named Letold and tripped over a helmet on the ground, falling over backward. Such a fall may seem fatal, but Hereward put it to good use, as he was now in the perfect position to attack Letold's undefended legs—which he did, cutting one leg clean off. Letold refused to yield and continued fighting on his knees until Hereward got bored with the fight and just left. Letold was in no position to pursue.

"The Wake" here just means "the watchful," and you can perceive that being watchful for opportunity is precisely what Hereward was good at.

A Maxim of the Fianna: Be no tale-bearer, nor utterer of falsehoods.

But sometimes you have to make your own opportunity. This, I have learned, is the Ultimate Fighting Technique, which I will now teach to you. Master this technique, and you will be able to defeat any regular knight in battle—and then we can move on to the weird stuff.

The Ultimate Fighting Technique: Its origin

The Ultimate Fighting Technique (which you will only learn here) was invented by Ireland's deadliest fighter, **Cúchulainn**. If you fail to master any other technique, this one will serve you well.

In his youth, Cúchulainn was training under the great Scottish warrior **Scáthach** when Scáthach was at war with her sister, **Aife**. At Scáthach's behest, Cúchulainn agreed to fight Aife in single combat while balanced on a tightrope strung over an abyss. But before he went to the fight, Cúchulainn asked Scáthach what her sister valued the most in the world.

Scáthach answered that most precious to Aife were her chariot, her charioteer, and the horses that pulled her chariot.

Cúchulainn faced off against Aife on the rope, and Aife immediately shattered his sword with one blow of her own. Cúchulainn was left defenseless. But he had the ultimate technique.

"Great googly moogly!" Cúchulainn shouted. "Aife, look, your chariot and your charioteer and your horses are all going off a cliff!"

Aife turned around to look for her beloved chariot, and Cúchulainn grabbed her and popped her into a sack. She later ransomed her life, but only by agreeing never to fight against Scáthach again.

The Ultimate Fighting Technique: Its refinement

A few centuries later, **Conán mac Morna**, one of the great representatives of our noble House Pismire (ah! sweet memories!) took Cúchulainn's Ultimate Technique and refined it, transforming what was already a thing of beauty into a radiant jewel of inestimable worth. My hat is off to you, Conán mac Morna!

The problem with Cúchulainn's method was simply that it required advance research. Aife was a chariot-lovin' lady, and if Scáthach hadn't known that about her sister, Cúchulainn would have been reduced to making guesses. "Aife, look, your Fabergé egg collection is falling off a cliff!" It would not have worked at all.

But Conán mac Morna once had to fight a pirate captain named Liagan; nothing else is known about Liagan: what he collected, what he loved. Conán's improvisation was elegant. Liagan was trash-talking (as pirates will) and belittling Conán's appearance. "You don't look so tough," and such statements. "Arrr."

"Indeed," said Conán mac Morna. "You probably have more to fear from the fellow behind you than from me."

Liagan looked behind him, and Conán cut him in two.

Unfortunately, Conán mac Morna employed his trick in full view of all the Fianna, those tree-dwelling do-gooders, while Cúchulainn was alone with Aife on a tightrope. That is why Cúchulainn is several hundred times more famous than Conán mac Morna.

Nevertheless, if you're ever in danger, it is Conán's technique you will probably want to employ.

Some Rules of Thumb

- Avoid fighting bandits, since bandits are just land pirates, and pirates are cooler and more interesting. Save your effort for pirates!

- At the start of any fight, you might want to exclaim, "Oh dear! My fifth combat of the day, and I have barely had time to recover from the last four! Ah, well, what can you do?"

- If you fight some unarmed peasants, maybe don't talk about it later, especially if you lose but also if you win.

- There's never any shame in saying, "You stay right here; I'm just going to go get my good sword, which I left in my other scabbard."

Cúchulainn's Other Fighting Techniques

Cúchulainn and other warriors from ancient Ireland learned various *cles*, or "feats" to use in combat. There are a lot of them, but some include:

The Apple Feat: The warrior juggles nine balls (or apples), keeping eight in the air and one in their hand at any given moment. This gives the warrior nine missiles that can be hurled in rapid succession. Cúchulainn was once practicing the Apple Feat when he was surprise attacked by his enemy Cûr macDa Loth; Cúchulainn threw the ball in his hand so hard it punctured Cûr's shield and passed through his head, making an apple-size hole in his brain.

The Edge Feat: Ancient Irish shields came with sharpened edges, and by holding the shield horizontally and swinging it, a warrior could use it as a weapon. When enemies cast their spears at Cúchulainn, he would counter with the Edge Feat, catching the spear points on his shield edge and deflecting them. In this way, his shield did not get weighed down by all the spears sticking into it.

The Salmon Leap: One of Cúchulainn's most commonly used feats. He would perform the Salmon Leap in order to attack an enemy from above, or to fight a giant face-to-face.

The Stroke of Precision: With this feat, a warrior could humiliate an opponent without actually doing harm, slicing off the enemy's hair, or even, with a few Strokes of Precision, removing their clothes. Always hilarious.

The Running-Up-a-Spear-and-Standing-Tiptoe-on-Its-Point Feat: This feat doesn't have as cool a name as the others, but you can imagine how demoralizing it must have been to the other side when a warrior performed it in battle.

The Gáe Bolga: The Gáe Bolga was both the name of Cúchulainn's special spear and the name of the feat that let him use it. No one but Cúchulainn ever mastered this particular feat.

None of these are as important as the Ultimate Fighting Technique, but of course each is useful in its own way. The Salmon Leap can help you get cookies off a high shelf, for example.

Other, less ultimate, fighting techniques

Skarphedinn once came across his enemy, Thrainn Sigfusson, while Thrainn was crossing an iced-over river with some friends. Skarphedinn was outnumbered, but he charged forward anyway. He was carrying his long-handled ax named Rimmugygr, which roughly translates as "The Ogress of War," and as he approached Thrainn, Skarphedinn slid on the ice on his smooth-soled boots. He skidded right past Thrainn, swinging Rimmugygr as he went. He must have had a lot of momentum, because the great ax cut Thrainn's skull in half at the jaw so that his teeth fell out and bounced on the ice. Before Thrainn's friends could even do anything beyond gaping at the sight of the bouncing teeth, Skarphedinn had slid away to the far bank of the river.

This technique only works on ice, but Skarphedinn lived in Iceland, so presumably he had plenty of opportunities to refine it. He must have gone back after and picked up the teeth because some time later, when some jerk named Gunnar Lambason was taunting him from a distance, Skarphedinn threw one of Thrainn's teeth at him and knocked out his eye, which is also a good, if not ultimate, fighting technique.

When your mother said you might put your eye out, she probably didn't mean with a dead man's tooth—but it could happen!

> "Richard raught him with a bar of brass
> That he caught at the gate.
> He broke his legs, he cried 'alas'
> And fell all check-mate."
>
> —*Sowdone of Babylone* (ca. 1400)

Bhima, the strongest of the five Pandava brothers, used to grab his opponents in battle and crush their bones and smoosh their bodies into the form of a sphere, whereupon he could just roll them away from him harmlessly.

Miyamoto Musashi writes in *The Book of Five Rings* about the technique of "gluing." This is when you block your opponent's sword and then keep your sword closely pressed against theirs, as though the two weapons were glued together, giving you the opportunity to move in closer safely.

But what if you actually covered your sword with glue? Wouldn't that work even better? I'm just spitballing here.

Finally, **Harishikha**, the son of a general from northern India, perfected a technique by which he could spin his spear so fast that it created a shield in front of him, one that could deflect hails of arrows. Harishikha could ride into combat on an elephant, spinning a spear of sufficient length that it protected both him and his mount, and no arrow could get past his defense. This is the kind of thing I would not believe was possible, had not someone else seen it with his own eyes and put it in a book I read part of.

Jousting

You're going to spend many a so-called "lab session" double period practicing jousting, at first just gripping your lance while you ride and then working your way up to jousting with a straw dummy. Your instructors will say, "Hold your shield a little in front of you, barely touching the horse's neck blah blah" and "cross the lance over your body pointing at blah blah blah," and I'm bored just writing it.

Jousting is not only dull, it's also dangerous. King Henry II of France went sport jousting with friends one summer day in 1559, and when a lance shattered against his shield (as it's supposed to), one small splinter of wood flew through the eyehole of his helmet and into his eye. Henry II lingered in agony for ten days before the splinter worked its way up through the eye and into his brain. Whatever safety precautions the Apprentice Academy has set up for its students, I can assure you that they are less rigorous than the precautions set up for the King of France, and even those didn't save Henry. Jousting is one of those things, like flossing, that's not even worth trying to do.

But if you must joust (and, to graduate, you must) — I will tell you the secret to jousting. This is precisely what your instructors will not tell you, but what you must do is begin throwing yourself backward off your saddle before your opponent's lance even comes in contact with your shield. The lance will strike with much less force, and you'll scarcely be winded when you hit the ground. The rules of jousting forbid a knight from sticking a lance into an opponent when they're down, so for the moment you'll be perfectly safe.

A Maxim of the Fianna: Stick to thy gear; hold fast to thy arms till the stern fight with its weapon-glitter be ended.

I called this the secret to jousting, but it's really the secret to opting out of jousting. If your opponent dismounts and comes by to fight, you can always play dead and, when they get too close, swing your sword. I'm not in charge of what you do. Your instructor probably won't like this, but you can always play dead and, when they get too close . . .

I believe **Manas** used this technique.

Freakish powers

It's bad enough that knights have swords and arrows and lances and things. Some knights are also blessed with freakish powers, which kind of sounds like cheating, honestly. If you can get some freakish

powers yourself, you should do that, but next best is learning how to counter others' freakish powers.

The blunting gaze: Aslak

The Jomsviking known as **Aslak Holmskalli** had the power to blunt all swords and axes just by looking at them. This worked great for him for a while. Opponents would go to an anvil and hammer their swords into a razor-sharp edge and then turn around to face Aslak, and those same swords were now blunt practice weapons. As long as he made sure not to look at his own sword, Aslak would win every fight every time.

How to counter this power: The remedy was discovered by the overmuscled **Vigfus Vigaglumsson**, who decided to cut out the middleman. Instead of using the anvil to sharpen his sword, he just carried the anvil into battle and threw it at Aslak. Aslak's piercing gaze—the opposite of a piercing gaze, really—watched as the anvil sailed through the air and crushed his skull.

Berserking: Cúchulainn

Some people—and you know who you are—have the power to go berserk in combat. *Berserk* just means *absolutely bonkers*. Berserkers wear no armor or, often, any clothes at all. They chew on their shields. When they are in a rage, they can feel neither fire nor steel, and cannot tell friend from foe, chopping everyone up indiscriminately. The Viking **Angantyr** and his eleven brothers were all berserkers, and when they felt the rages coming on, they would run out into the woods and wrestle with trees and rocks, just so they wouldn't end up killing one another.

Doubtless the worst berserk fury of all belonged to **Cúchulainn**. When he went into his rage—he called it a "warp-spasm"—his whole body became distorted. His feet and knees twisted around so they faced backward.

When a berserker was chewing his shield while facing off against **Grettir the Strong**, Grettir kicked the shield and shattered the berserker's jaw.

His mouth stretched from ear to ear, and he opened it wide enough that you could look down and see his lungs fluttering. One of his eyes sank so deep into his skull that the long beak of a crane couldn't have plucked it back out, while the other eye swelled up and popped out, dangling from its socket and larger than a fist.

(In my sources this horrible description goes on for several paragraphs, but I don't even want to think about what happens to his teeth, so I'll stop here.)

Attempting to calm down from his warp-spasm, Cúchulainn would plunge into three vats of ice water, one after the other. The first vat would burst from the steam, the second would boil over, and the third would end up lukewarm. By this point, the warp-spasm was over.

How to counter this power: You should be waiting in a fourth vat of ice water.

Invulnerability: Sigurd/Achilles/Ferdiad

Sigurd bathed in dragon's blood and came out with skin that no weapon could pierce—**Achilles** was dipped in the river Styx and came out with skin that no weapon could pierce—**Ferdiad** . . . well, I don't know how Ferdiad did it, but he had skin like horn, which no weapon could pierce.

How to counter this power: It always works out that invulnerable people have One Weak Point.

Achilles had his proverbial heel, where his mother held him when she dipped him in the river, and indeed some guy named Paris shot him with an arrow just there.

Sigurd was vulnerable between his shoulders.

In Ferdiad's case, since his skin was as strong as animal horn, the only weak spot was his butthole, which was of course hard to hit because he would never let anyone get behind him in combat. When Ferdiad fought **Cúchulainn** at a ford in a stream, he was for a long time winning—until Cúchulainn's charioteer floated the Gáe Bolga, Cúchulainn's deadly spear, down the stream. It floated down to Cúchulainn, who grabbed it between his toes. Cúchulainn feinted with another spear, and, while Ferdiad was dodging, Cúchulainn lifted the Gáe Bolga with his toes, striking Ferdiad from below—and that was the end of Ferdiad.

How did they find out where Sigurd was vulnerable? Sigurd's friends, who were actually his enemies, asked his wife to mark his clothing with a little cross over any vulnerable spots so they could protect those in battle with especial care. Needless to say, once they saw where the sole cross was—that was the end of Sigurd.

Sort of like invulnerability: Atli the Short

Iron could not bite the skin of **Atli the Short**. Some people said it was because he was a berserker, and berserkers (as we mentioned) could not feel the bite of iron. **Egil Skallagrimsson** theorized it was because he had a gaze like Aslak's, and such a gaze (as we mentioned) could blunt any weapon. Or maybe he just had something in the Sigurd/Achilles/Ferdiad vein. We'll probably never find out the truth, because Atli died a thousand years ago.

How to counter this power: Egil Skallagrimsson himself figured it out. When he fought Atli, he just threw away his sword, wrestled the man to the ground, and used his teeth to tear out Atli's throat. Easy-peasy. Of course, it's a little disgusting, but Egil was hardly someone to avoid being a little disgusting. He once ate so much at a banquet that he realized he was going to vomit; he knew that everyone would make fun of him if he did; so he went up to his host, grabbed him by the shoulders, and threw up right in the poor guy's face.

The grossed-out host began vomiting, too, of course. And Egil turned to everyone and said, "I can hardly be blamed for throwing up. I'm doing no more than our host has done."

If you can live your entire life as a disgusting slob, biting someone's throat out should be no problem. I speak from experience.

Solar strength: Gawain

Sir Gawain's strength was tied to the position of the sun. It would wax throughout the morning, until at noon he was invincible in battle. After noon, though, his strength would wane, and by the middle of the night he had only normal human strength.

How to counter this power: Obviously, it's best to fight Gawain at night—but he'll be ready for this. If you can, surprise him by fighting him at noon *right before a solar eclipse*.

Strange bear powers: Bödvar

Bödvar, warrior in the employ of the Danish king **Hrolf Kraki**, had a father who was a literal bear (actually a human who had been turned into a bear by magical wolfskin gloves), so he himself had Strange Bear Powers. He could go into a trance and manifest a gigantic bear spirit. While his body lay there senseless, the giant bear would roam around mauling opponents and routing armies.

How to counter this power: Just wake him up. Once Bödvar was out of the trance, the bear spirit would disappear . . . which is what happened in Hrolf Kraki's last battle. When his kingdom was besieged

28

by trolls and zombies, the only thing holding them off was Bödvar's bear spirit. But Bödvar's buddy, **Hjalti**, noticing that Bödvar wasn't on the front lines, went back to the castle, where he found Bödvar's body in a trance.

"Wake up, you coward!" Hjalti said. "There's a battle going on outside."

And Bödvar woke up, the bear spirit disappeared from the battlefield, and trolls and zombies overran the kingdom, killing everyone.

So it's too late for Bödvar, but remember this for the next son of a bear who brings a gigantic bear spirit to battle.

Decavirile strength: Galahad

Sir Galahad famously had the strength of ten men, "because," he'd explain, "my heart is pure."

How to counter this power: Get him an internet connection.

Wait! These are all knight vs. knight combats! What if I'm fighting a sorcerer?

There is perhaps an inherent conflict of interest in my advising you about fighting sorcerers. I try to be impartial. Nevertheless, I have to admit that sorcerers are simply really bad at fighting knights, and you'll probably do fine. They may look very impressive with their levitation and pyrotechnics, but when the chips are down, sorcerers always choke.

This is how it goes. The Bogatyr **Alyosha Popovich** was once set to fight the sorcerer Tugarin. Tugarin had magic wings made of paper with which he could hover above the combat and drop spells down on his helpless foes below. So Alyosha simply waited to fight Tugarin . . . when it was raining! The hapless wizard's paper wings disintegrated and Tugarin fell to his death. Aloysha didn't even have to draw his sword.

Bradamante, the Paladin, fought a sorcerer named Atlantes and just pretended she was fooled by all his illusions. Finally, she fell down, perhaps shouting, "Ugh! You got me!" When he bent over to take her unconscious form prisoner . . . well, look, you know this trick. This is a good trick. Bradamante chained Atlantes up and got him to release all the scads of other knights he'd imprisoned. Don't worry about sorcerers. There are plenty of other things to worry about, such as cursed swords or large boars.

Wait! I thought of something to worry about!
These are all knight vs. human combats!
What if I'm fighting a dragon or something?

There's no need to be alarmed. This book is designed to answer every question you've ever had on any topic. For example: Katina Paxinou. Bismarck. Three. A topical ointment.

In this case, the answer to your specific question is *on the next page*.

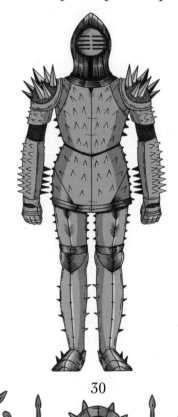

Fighting Dragons

EVENTUALLY, OF COURSE, YOU'LL WANT TO STOP KILLING OTHER KNIGHTS and start killing monsters. It's more impressive, for one thing. And naturally, the top deed of choice for any self-respecting knight is killing dragons. You only need to ice one dragon before you get the nickname "dragon slayer," and once you get a nickname like that, you're set. You never have to do a lick of work again for the rest of your life.

The usual way to fight a dragon (and the one your instructors will favor, the fools) is to charge at it with couched lance. This is the worst idea you could possibly have. If one guy with a pointy stick could defeat a dragon, we'd hardly have all these dragons around, would we? Dragons have a name for a charging knight, and that name is *food*. Charge a dragon and learn what it's like to be lower down the food chain.

Dragons tend to breathe either fire or poison. Many can fly, and those that can't fly have long, sinuous bodies that they can wrap around you, python style, crushing you to death. Some have poisonous stingers in their tail. This is all pretty bad, but on the plus side, they do collect enormous mounds of gold. Only on a bed of cooling, soothing gold can they rest comfortably—because *a dragon's blood is boiling hot, bubbling like acid, and usually poisonous!*

If you can kill such a dragon with your little lance, you hardly need this book. But for everyone else, let us turn our attention to some of the cunning methods those who have weaseled before us have used.

What method to use depends on the kind of dragon you encounter.

If the dragon be sinuous → use the Loschy method:

Peter Loschy was a knight from Yorkshire, England, who decided to purge the countryside of a certain snake-like dragon that had been slithering around poisoning crops and eating locals with impunity.

He had special armor made with razor-sharp spikes sticking out all over. When the dragon came to wrap itself around Loschy, it merely impaled itself on the spikes. With the dragon bleeding out, and conveniently held in one place, Loschy was then able to chop the beast up. When the dragon pieces started to reattach themselves, re-forming its serpentine body, Loschy's faithful dog quickly grabbed the chunks of dragon flesh in its jaws and buried them in various secret places around Yorkshire.

Spiked armor is difficult to walk in and tends to cause a lot of accidents. Try to scratch yourself in the wrong place, and you'll end up impaled on your own armor, which is always humiliating. If your mother tries to give you a congratulatory hug after you dispatch a dragon, you will find that you have also dispatched your mother. Also, armor tricked out with spikes is ludicrously expensive, and like a bridesmaid's dress, you can only really wear it once. For all these reasons, you might want to try the bargain-basement Loschy method used by the Viking **Ragnar Loth-brok** (or "Hairy-britches"). He put on shaggy fur pants and then waded through icy water until the fur on the pants froze into hairy icicles. When sundry serpents tried to wind around his legs, they pierced themselves. All Ragnar had to do was stand by a fire, and his thawing pants were back to normal and suitable for daily wear.

One word of caution: Peter Loschy's tale has a tragic ending, for, after the dragon was dismembered and buried, said faithful dog gave its master's face a lick. The poison inherent in the dragon chunks had permeated the dog's slobber, which killed Loschy, and then the dog. If you are going to all the trouble of preparing armor with spikes, perhaps also invest in a couple of sticks so you can play fetch with your dog, keeping it at a distance until the poison works itself through its system.

If the dragon have boiling blood → use the Sigurd method:

Sigurd was the son of the great hero **Sigmund**, sent to be raised by a foster father (as was the custom at the time) named Regin. Unbeknownst to everyone, Regin's brother was a literal dragon, in fact the largest dragon then living, a great wyrm known as Fafnir, and Regin sicced Sigurd on him. Sigurd was the greatest warrior in Europe, or at least he had been since the day **Beowulf** charged at a dragon himself, but even Sigurd had no chance against Fafnir in a fair fight.

I don't need to tell you that fair fights have no place in the repertoire of a true knight.

Fafnir's blood ran so hot that not only did he need to sleep on a record-setting mountain of gold, he also made frequent trips to a nearby lake to guzzle water. A dragon

33

the size of Fafnir, dragging its dragon belly between a cave and a lake, leaves an obvious track, and it was along this track that Sigurd prepared some trenches. First he dug a pit deep enough to crouch in. Then he dug two shallower channels leading away from him. He waited in the pit, facing backward, until Fafnir passed overhead . . . and then he simply stuck his sword into Fafnir's weak underside. With the sword held in place, Fafnir's own momentum tore a long, gaping wound into the dragon's belly.

Of course, boiling blood came gushing out: But Sigurd had dug channels for the blood to flow down, so the wave of blood never rolled back into the pit he stood in.

After the blood had cooled down, Sigurd bathed in it, which made his skin hard as steel—except for one place between his shoulder blades, where a leaf, adhering to his back, left the skin unhardened. If you're going to bathe in dragon's blood, *always check for leaves*.

Digging a Trench

Death from Below is one of the most reliable methods of dragon slaying, but you do need to have the pits dug before the dragon comes wandering by. Nothing's more embarrassing than being caught with a shovel instead of a sword by a hungry dragon.

To dig fast:

1. Dig a shallow outline of the trench you want to dig.
2. Carry water (from the nearby lake!) and pour it into your trench.
3. Cover the trench with reeds or sticks and let it sit overnight.
4. When you return, the water will be gone, and the soil at the bottom of your trench will be loose and easy to dig fast. Dig until the soil is hard, then repeat steps *2* through *4* again until the trench is done.

If the dragon breathe fire and can fly →
use the Alexander method:

Alexander the Great conquered the world, and I can assure you he didn't do it by charging at dragons and getting eaten. While adventuring deep in the western lands, Alexander learned of a dragon that lived atop an inaccessible mountain. Every day, the locals left five cows at the foot of the mountain as a free meal. As long as the dragon got its cows, it would not fly out and torch the surrounding towns—but the locals were running low on cows!

Dragonfighting tip: If you can, try (as the Persian hero **Sam**, "most exalted of the mighty men," did) shooting an arrow through a dragon's jaws, piercing them both and clamping them shut. No way for the dragon to breathe fire or swallow Sam whole with its jaws held shut!

Thinking quickly, Alexander ordered that five of the remaining cows be killed and skinned, and the skins stuffed like balloons with venom and oil. He left the dummy cows in the usual place, and, lo, the dragon came down and swallowed the cows like little pills. First the venom flooded the dragon's system, and then the oil made contact with the dragon's internal flame. If the dragon wasn't killed by the poison, it sure was by the explosion.

If the dragon be a lady transformed by her wicked stepmother → use the Kemp Owyne method

"The warst woman that ever lived" (the ballad says) changed her stepdaughter Isabel into a dragon whose very skin was deadly poison to the touch. A dragon she needs must remain until kissed three times, which you will perceive is challenging with all that poison skin.

Isabel searched beneath the waves (where magic items often end up) until she found a magical belt, a magical ring, and a magical sword that would protect from all poison whoever held them. Then she gave them to a knight she liked, one **Kemp Owyne**, who promptly kissed her three times, breaking the spell.

If the transformed dragon does not have at the ready three magic items to protect from poison . . . I don't know, maybe tell the dragon to go look for them.

I probably should have called this "the Isabel method," but I hate naming things after dragons.

Other Famous Dragon Slayers

George:
The most
celebrated
of dragon
slayers,
a Roman
soldier who
fought his
dragon in
Libya and
was sainted
for his
troubles.

Sir Tristram: Traveled all the way to Ireland to slay a dragon.

Rostam: While Rostam slept, a dragon tried to creep up on him. Fortunately, his wonder horse Rakhsh was there to wake him up . . . but by the time the horse roused Rostam, the dragon slipped out of sight. This happened several times, and Rakhsh was in serious danger of getting brained by an angry, sleepy Rostam, before the dragon proved too slow in retreat and the hero caught a glimpse of it. After that, the rest was easy: Rostam rode the dragon down and slew it.

Beowulf: Said dragon was the last thing he ever slew.

Salur Kazan: On an unsuccessful hunting trip in Turkestan, Salur Kazan prayed for game—and beware of what you wish for because all of a sudden up came a seven-headed dragon (which, fortunately, Salur Kazan was able to dispatch).

Bahram Gur: "That great hunter" Bahram traveled from Persia to India to fight rhinoceroses and ended up killing a dragon there by shooting it with arrows dipped in poison and milk.

Menestratos: Menestratos put on spiked armor, à la Peter Loschy, and then . . . jumped down the dragon's throat? Yeah, I guess it worked, insofar as it spelled the end of the dragon, but it also spelled the end of Menestratos. Not recommended!

Sir Lancelot: "There came out an horrible and a fiendly dragon, spitting fire out of his mouth. Then Sir Launcelot drew his sword and fought with the dragon long, and at the last with great pain Sir Launcelot slew that dragon" (reports Sir Thomas Malory).

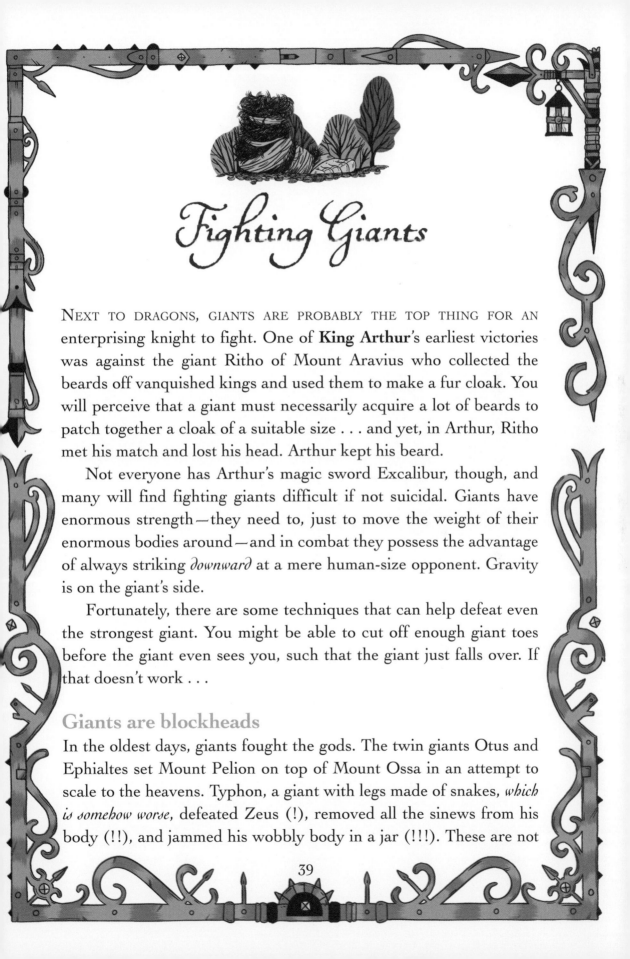

Fighting Giants

NEXT TO DRAGONS, GIANTS ARE PROBABLY THE TOP THING FOR AN enterprising knight to fight. One of **King Arthur**'s earliest victories was against the giant Ritho of Mount Aravius who collected the beards off vanquished kings and used them to make a fur cloak. You will perceive that a giant must necessarily acquire a lot of beards to patch together a cloak of a suitable size . . . and yet, in Arthur, Ritho met his match and lost his head. Arthur kept his beard.

Not everyone has Arthur's magic sword Excalibur, though, and many will find fighting giants difficult if not suicidal. Giants have enormous strength—they need to, just to move the weight of their enormous bodies around—and in combat they possess the advantage of always striking *downward* at a mere human-size opponent. Gravity is on the giant's side.

Fortunately, there are some techniques that can help defeat even the strongest giant. You might be able to cut off enough giant toes before the giant even sees you, such that the giant just falls over. If that doesn't work . . .

Giants are blockheads

In the oldest days, giants fought the gods. The twin giants Otus and Ephialtes set Mount Pelion on top of Mount Ossa in an attempt to scale to the heavens. Typhon, a giant with legs made of snakes, *which is somehow worse*, defeated Zeus (!), removed all the sinews from his body (!!), and jammed his wobbly body in a jar (!!!). These are not the kind of guys you're going to be able to take down with a shot to the toe. There's no fighting these guys.

Fortunately, giants are not the brightest, and when you can't fight 'em, you can trick 'em. A few tricks that have worked in the past from A.A. alumni . . .

Jack is the all-time greatest of giant killers. Not the Jack with a beanstalk (though he killed a giant, too). I'm talking about *Jack*! Jack *the Giant Killer*! He had enough weasely tricks to fill a whole chapbook.

So there was this one time Jack got into a porridge-eating contest with a Welsh giant, which, you will note, sounds foolish. Giants can really pack their food away! Jack, however, had supplied himself with a leather bag, which he secreted under his shirt. As the giant was shoveling porridge down his gullet, Jack just shoveled porridge under his collar and into the leather bag, matching the giant spoonful for spoonful.

When they were done (it was a tie!), Jack showed the giant another trick he could do. With his clasp knife he cut right through his shirt and the leather bag, spilling all the porridge back out onto the table. Now he could eat it again!

"Well, if you can get your porridge back that way, then surely I can as well," said the giant, and he picked up his own, larger knife.

That was one less giant in Wales.

Finn Mac Cool, leader of the Fianna, once learned that a Scottish giant named Benandonner was crossing over to Ireland, looking for both trouble and Finn. Aware that Benandonner was too large to fight, Finn and his wife Sadhbh hatched a plan.

First Sadhbh dressed Finn as a baby. When Benandonner came to the Mac Cool house, Sadhbh told the giant that this large, muscular man was her newborn son. The giant was impressed by the size of baby Mac Cool and began to worry that his father might be tough to tackle. Then Sadhbh fed the baby a loaf of white bread and offered Benandonner another loaf. But instead of bread,

she passed him a white rock. The giant took one bite and broke his teeth.

"How odd," Sadhbh said. "That's my husband's favorite meal." The giant took one look at the baby, who was noshing the food the giant had failed to eat, and began to panic. "Anyway," Sadhbh went on, "Finn should be back home any minute now . . ."

And with that, the giant ran back to Scotland.

One more example: I don't even know who this guy was, but **some cobbler** met a giant who was on his way to destroy the town of Shrewsbury. The giant asked him how far he had to walk to reach his goal, and the cobbler, in reply, opened up his pack filled with dozens of pairs of worn-out shoes (which, of course, being a cobbler, he had been collecting to mend).

"I've just come from Shrewsbury," lied the cobbler, "and the way was so long I wore through all of these shoes."

Deciding that that was just too far of a journey, the giant turned back, presumably to destroy some other town instead.

Special techniques against giants

» Corsolt

Count Guillaume Shortnose fought the giant Corsolt (this was the battle that shortened his nose) and found that the giant's armor was too strong for his sword to cut—and the giant's unprotected face was too far away to reach! Guillaume got battered so badly, Corsolt assumed he was dead. But he wasn't, and when the giant bent down to pick up the battered body, Guillaume hacked his skull in two with a blow to the face.

A Maxim of the Fianna: In a great man's household be quiet; be surly in the narrow pass.

Remember, the **Bradamante** trick of *playing possum* is a good technique against almost any opponent, but you can see how it has extra benefits with giants.

41

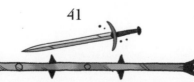

≫ Antaeus

Hercules (who was, no offense, probably stronger than you) wrestled a giant named Antaeus, the son of the Gaia, the earth. Whenever Antaeus touched his mother, he found his strength always renewing and increasing, and since wrestling moves tend to throw an opponent to the ground . . . well, wrestling Antaeus was a losing proposition. Every time you threw him down successfully, he just got stronger!

Finally, Hercules figured out the problem and lifted Antaeus up. Now he lacked all contact with the earth, and became weak and helpless as a kitten, or at least weak and helpless as an ordinary giant, which meant he was no match for Hercules, who just crushed him to powder in his strong grip.

Lifting a giant off the ground is not a simple task—you can't grab him around the waist to lift him up, as you might a normal person, because he's a giant. You're lucky if, on tiptoe, you can reach his waist. Instead, you have to grab him by the ankles, a hold that does not give the lifter much leverage. There are about four thousand old-timey sculptures depicting this wrestling match, and none of them are much use because in none of them does Antaeus look particularly *giant*.

It might be easier (should you ever face an Antaeus) to lift him up with a pulley or a crane.

≫ Hilde

The giantess Hilde, meanwhile, had the power to regenerate from any wound. **Dietrich of Bern**, when he dueled her, kept chopping the giantess in half . . . and her two halves just snapped back together. Finally, Dietrich realized that after he bisected Hilde, he should jump in between the two pieces before they joined again . . . and that did the trick.

If you ever manage to chop a giant in two, it's not a bad idea to try jumping between the two pieces, just in case. It can't hurt!

42

Unless they snap back together when you're in between them. That would be gross. So jump fast!

» Some giantess near an island off Norway

The Viking **Arrow-Odd** once spotted a hostile giantess wading through the sea, approaching his island home. Fortunately, he had killed and skinned a bear some time earlier, so he hastily propped the bear skin up with a stick and placed hot coals in its gaping mouth. As smoke issued from the bear's mouth, Arrow-Odd stood behind the bear skin with his bow. He shot an arrow—right through the bear skin—at the giantess. Fortunately, she was too large a target to miss, as he was firing blind. Unfortunately, all she had to do was hold up one massive hand, and the arrow pricked it with no more force than a dust mote.

Now Arrow-Odd had a quiver full of magical arrows called *Gusisnautar*—they're what put the *Arrow* in the name *Arrow-Odd*—and he fired one of these through the bear skin. Again the giantess held up her hand to block the incoming missile, but the magical arrow pierced the hand, flew on and struck her eye, coming out the other side of her head. Even with her great size, such a wound had to smart. When another magical arrow flew through the bear skin, once again shooting through the giantess's body, she turned back and reported to her king that the island was populated by fire-breathing monsters that shot pain from a distance. No giant bothered Arrow-Odd after that.

» The giant's heart

Many giants achieve a kind of immortality by keeping their heart far away from their body, and fighting such opponents can be especially tricky.

According to Scottish legend, the **queen of Easaidh Ruadh** was once kidnapped by a giant. She noticed that although her captor

44

would frequently get wounded, the wounds had no ill effect, and the giant explained, when she asked, that he could not be killed because he kept his heart outside his body, in the baking stone. The next time the giant left his castle, the captive queen cleaned and polished the baking stone.

The giant, returning, was pleased to see what she had done. But he explained that he actually kept his heart under the front threshold, and not in the baking stone at all. So the queen busied herself sweeping and tidying the threshold.

"Well, well!" said the giant. "You really will take good care of my heart!" And then he told her that actually, *actually* under a nearby flagstone there was a sheep, and inside the sheep was a duck, and inside the duck was an egg, and in that egg was the giant's heart.

The next time the giant left, the queen overturned the flagstone, purged the sheep, de-egged the duck, and crushed the egg in her hand. Then she returned, free, to Easaidh Ruadh.

It turns out that keeping their hearts outside their bodies is something giants love to do. It's common enough that, before you try fighting a giant, you should check to make sure you're actually fighting something you should stab. It is, in fact, easiest to kill a giant if you can do it by digging up a flagstone or two and never meeting the big fellow face-to-face.

I cannot say I approve of the queen of Easaidh Ruadh's actions. She should have found the corpse of the giant, cut its head off, and carried it back to town, bragging she'd slain it in single combat. A missed opportunity! Was the queen of Easaidh Ruadh even a graduate of the Apprentice Academy? (It's impossible to tell because her name is lost.)

Other Famous Giant Slayers

David: You know, the whole sling trick.

Sir Tristram: He slew the giant Nabon, lord of the Isle of Servage, and handed the island over to a friend of his, Sir Segwarides. The moral of this story is *make friends with Tristram.*

Thomas Hickathrift: Looking for a weapon long enough to hit a giant's head, he used a cart axle. When the axle broke, he picked up a very tall man by the feet and beat the giant to a pulp with that poor fellow. The moral here is *don't stand near Thomas Hickathrift.*

Warzameg: The Nart Warzameg slew that scaly giant Arkhon Arkhozh . . . but you've probably already read all about that in some other book.

Tom Thumb: In the days of King Arthur, Tom Thumb spent his time fighting giants, which is a little weird because everyone was, like, a giant compared to Tom Thumb.

Basat: This Turkish hero killed the man-eating one-eyed giant Tepegöz, whose magic ring made its skin invulnerable, by attacking its eye, and then stealing the blind creature's ring . . . leaving it vulnerable to decapitation.

Odysseus: Another eye thing, another blinding, which really skeeves me out. Technically, Odysseus didn't kill the cyclops Polyphemus, but I'll count it.

Sir Lancelot: "Anon withal came there upon him two great giants, well armed all save the heads, with two horrible clubs in their hands. Sir Launcelot put his shield afore him and put the stroke away of the one giant, and with his sword he clave his head asunder. When his fellow saw that, he ran away as he were wood [crazed], for fear of the horrible strokes, and Launcelot after him with all his might, and smote him on the shoulder, and clave him to the navel" (reports Sir Thomas Malory).

Giant allies

Of course the best thing is to befriend a giant and get that giant to do the fighting for you! Even though the Apprentice Academy rather shamefacedly never mentions this fact, the truth is that House Biscione has had many giants graduate under its auspices, and House Escallop has seen a few, too. If you, yourself, dear reader, are a giant, please take no offense at the preceding pages. Instead, stand tall, so to speak, with pride, as we salute some of the Apprentice Academy's great larger-than-life graduates!

≫ Aadi Madi-Karib

Aadi was a bandit defeated by, and later allied with, the great Arab warrior **Amir Hamza**. Aadi's prodigious strength and size (thirty-one feet tall, by one estimate), as well as his outsize appetite, served Hamza well on his adventures. During one campaign against the king of Egypt, Hamza, Aadi, and their friends took over the royal palace, but sought the king of Egypt high and low in vain. Unable to find the king, Aadi decided to pause and have a meal. He ate so much of the king's fruit, he finally had to visit the royal outhouse. It turned out that this was where the king was hiding. Like, down the hole in the outhouse, where no one had thought to look. But then Aadi sat down . . .

The alarmed king soon found himself almost buried in giant dung. Desperate to pull himself out, he reached up and grabbed Aadi in a delicate area. Aadi, surprised, leaped to his feet and ran naked through the palace, dragging the filthy king, holding on for dear life, behind him. "Help me, Hamza!" the giant cried. "I've pooped out the king of Egypt!"

In this way did they capture the king. Although they were hesitant to touch him.

It is convenient to have a giant as an ally, because: Would you want to have to do this yourself?

≫ Mac Cécht

Mac Cécht's sword was thirty feet long from point to haft, which sounds impossible to wield, except Mac Cécht was himself enormous. An enemy coming upon Mac Cécht as he lay down once mistook his eyes and nose for two lakes near a mountain. When he wasn't fighting with the sword, he used a white-hot iron bar, each blow of which could fell nine men. He served Conaire Mór, high king of Ireland.

At the battle of Da Derga's Hostel—a *hotel*, some people'd call it—Mac Cécht fought side by side with his king as the loyalist forces were besieged by pirates who surrounded the building. Prodigies of valor dealt by King Conaire Mór and his soldiers kept the pirates at bay, but, as the fighting dragged on, the king found himself perishing of thirst. All the water in the hostel had been used up putting out fires set by the besiegers, so the king asked Mac Cécht to go find him some water, to allow him to keep fighting.

Mac Cécht battled his way out of the hostel and strode across Ireland, cup in hand, looking for a draft. But this was the day of doom for King Conaire, and even the elements were against him. Every well, every river, every lake was dry. Finally, Mac Cécht found water in Lough Gara and filled the cup—but he was now some distance away from Da Derga's Hostel! He hurried back to the fight and arrived in time to see two pirates cutting Conaire's head off. Although one tried to run away with the severed head, Mac Cécht crushed the pirate by dropping a stone pillar on him. Then Mac Cécht grabbed his king's severed head and dutifully poured the cup of Lough Gara water down his throat. The fight was still going on, so Mac Cécht waded back into it until he fell, mortally wounded.

As he lay dying on the field of battle, Mac Cécht asked a passing woman what kind of biting insect was in his wound—a fly or a midge. The woman told him it was no fly but a wolf, gnawing deep into his body.

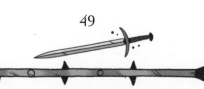

"Well, that's a surprise," Mac Cécht said as he died.

So fell the tallest of the high king's champions. You'll notice that when he was sent to get the king water, he did exactly what he was sent to do.

It is convenient to have a giant as an ally, because: A fellow does get thirsty sometimes.

King Arthur once "slew a great giant named Galapas, which was a man of an huge quantity and height. He shorted him and smote off both his legs by the knees, saying, 'Now art thou better of a size to deal with than thou were,' and after smote off his head."

» Svyatogor

Svyatogor the Bogatyr fought for Prince Vladimir of Kiev. He was large enough that his fellow Bogatyr, **Ilya Muromets**, once hid in his pocket; Svyatogor didn't even notice until his horse complained that carrying two heroes at once was too much.

In strength Svyatogor was unmatched in all the Kievan Empire, and perhaps in all of Europe at the time, Ilya notwithstanding. But we've already remarked that giants tend to be a little dim, and Svyatogor was no exception. One day, while adventuring with Ilya Muromets, Svyatogor came across an enormous stone coffin. Ilya tried it out for size, but it was of course far too big for merely a tall, strapping man. Svyatogor lay down in it, and indeed, he fit perfectly. He asked Ilya to put the lid on the coffin, and Ilya told

A Maxim of the Fianna: Two-thirds of thy gentleness be shown to women and to those that creep on the floor (little children) and to poets, and be not violent to the common people.

him not to be a dunce. But Svyatogor would have his will, and he got up and grabbed the lid himself, lying back down, setting the lid on top . . .

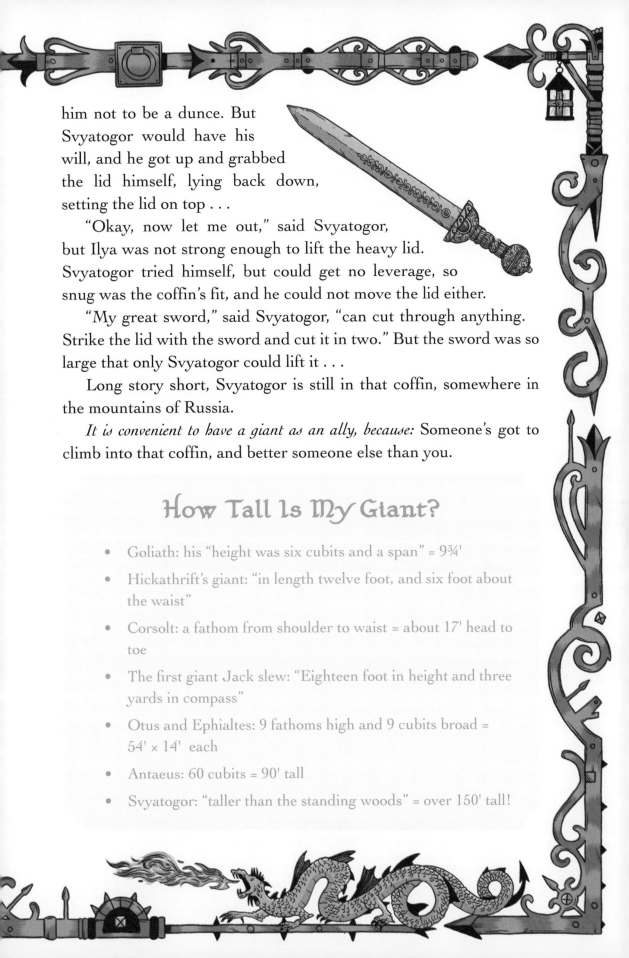

"Okay, now let me out," said Svyatogor, but Ilya was not strong enough to lift the heavy lid. Svyatogor tried himself, but could get no leverage, so snug was the coffin's fit, and he could not move the lid either.

"My great sword," said Svyatogor, "can cut through anything. Strike the lid with the sword and cut it in two." But the sword was so large that only Svyatogor could lift it . . .

Long story short, Svyatogor is still in that coffin, somewhere in the mountains of Russia.

It is convenient to have a giant as an ally, because: Someone's got to climb into that coffin, and better someone else than you.

How Tall Is My Giant?

- Goliath: his "height was six cubits and a span" = 9¾'
- Hickathrift's giant: "in length twelve foot, and six foot about the waist"
- Corsolt: a fathom from shoulder to waist = about 17' head to toe
- The first giant Jack slew: "Eighteen foot in height and three yards in compass"
- Otus and Ephialtes: 9 fathoms high and 9 cubits broad = 54' × 14' each
- Antaeus: 60 cubits = 90' tall
- Svyatogor: "taller than the standing woods" = over 150' tall!

What If This Happens to You?

If you ever get stuck in a coffin with a lid only you can lift . . . don't bother trying to use your arms. I mean, you can *try* using your arms, and if the lid is light enough it'll come right off. But you don't need a book to tell you to *push the lid off.* Instead:

1. Work your legs up over your chest, crisscross-applesauce. If the coffin be narrow, you'll have to do one leg at a time, but the principle is the same: Slide your leg up until it is bent at the knee over your abdomen.

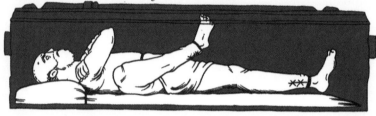

2. Now unkink your leg so that the foot is about even with your head. Unless you are naturally flexible, this should be *very uncomfortable.*

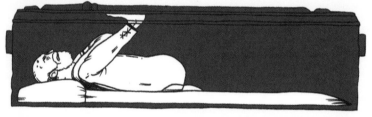

3. By rotating your leg, you can get your knee next to your body. If you cross your arms over your chest at the same time as you rotate your leg, your knee will be able to fit into the area your arm had been in, even inside a tight coffin. Now your feet are against the coffin lid.

4. Simply straighten your legs, and the lid will come off.

Now *don't fall for that again*!

52

» Rainouart

The Spanish giant **Rainouart** joined the forces of the French king Louis under the famous knight **Guillaume d'Orange**. And, sure, *it is convenient to have a giant as an ally, because* Rainouart was bigger and stronger than everyone else in the army, and he could take on a whole legion of enemies by himself.

But there are also . . . inconveniences.

1. Being no smarter than the average giant, Rainouart would often forget the enormous club he was wont to carry into battle. He would show up at the fight, and someone would say, "Rainouart, where's your club?" and then he'd facepalm, because the club was back at the castle. This kept happening.

No problem (you're probably thinking). *Just send someone back to fetch his club.* No offense to apprentice knights, but this is practically what a squire is for, after all.

Unfortunately, Rainouart's club was so large that it could only be drawn to the battlefield by a team of four horses. Fourteen strong men it took to hoist the darn thing into the cart in the first place.

2. And then Rainouart's great strength could sometimes be a little too great. In the middle of one battle in southern France, Guillaume's nephew **Sir Bertrand** had his horse killed beneath him. His friend Rainouart, standing nearby, offered to get Bertrand another horse, by a standard giant method—killing an enemy knight and taking his horse, naturally.

And indeed, one of the enemy came galloping along, lance couched for battle, and Rainouart just swung his great club, smashing the knight on the head . . . with such great strength that he squashed the horse like a potato.

Knight after knight came by, and Rainouart killed each of them, but each horse ended up dead as well, until Bertrand counseled Rainouart to swing his club sidearm, like a baseball bat, sweeping the enemy out of their saddle but leaving their horse untouched. A real waste of good horseflesh, all those previous downward swings.

3. Giants like Rainouart also have tempers. After a victory at the Battle of Aliscans, Rainouart arrived at the walled city of Orange much later than the other French knights—they all had horses, after all, while he had to walk. The French were celebrating inside the town, leaving no one to open the gate for Rainouart. At first the giant waited patiently. But as the evening wore on, he swore revenge—first against Guillaume, who was presumably feasting safe and warm in Orange, and then against King Louis, who was all the way back in Paris and could hardly be blamed. Rainouart had even set off on the long journey to Paris, with the explicit goal of murdering the king and tearing the whole city to pieces, but before he'd gotten too far along the road, Guillaume learned his ally had been left outside. A hard ride to catch up and at last Guillaume, after really very many apologies, managed to placate the giant.

But, yeah, sure, there are conveniences, too.

"Here Lubin listened with awe-struck surprise
When Hickathrift's great strength has met his ear;
How he kill'd giants as they were but flies,
And lifted trees as one would lift a spear,
Though not much bigger than his fellows were;
He knew no troubles wagoners have known,
Of getting stall'd and such disasters drear;
Up he'd chuck sacks as we would hurl a stone,
And draw whole loads of grain unaided and alone."

—Clare, "The Village Minstrel" (1821)

Fighting Boars

A SOOTHSAYER ONCE CAME ACROSS ARGONAUT ANCAEUS PLANTING A vineyard and prophesied that he would not live to drink of its produce. Some time later, **Ancaeus** had squeezed out the grapes and fermented some wine, and was about to drink a cup, when he paused. "Go get that soothsayer," he said. "I want him to see me take my first drink."

While he was waiting, a wild boar came along and gored him to death. The untasted wine spilled on the ground.

The point of this story may be to beware of soothsayers, but it is also definitely to *beware of boars*. Tigers and bears *sound* scarier, and dragons and giants *are* scarier, but boars are responsible for a good amount of trouble in the knightly tradition, and I would be remiss if I failed to address these beasts.

"A tusked boar, that is fearful for a man to see before him in the glens of a mountain, resolves to fight with the huntsmen and whets his white tusks, turning sideways, while foam flows all round his mouth as he gnashes, and his eyes are like glowing fire, and he bristles the hair on his mane and around his neck . . ."

—pseudo-Hesiod, *Aspis Herakleous* (sixth-century BC)

The Calydonian Boar

There was a year when the king of Calydon forgot to include the goddess Artemis in his yearly sacrifices, and let me tell you, in ancient Greece this was a very dangerous thing to forget. So Artemis, in revenge, sent an oversize boar to ravage the countryside.

The king's son, **Meleager**, was not going to take this lying down. He called all the great heroes of Greece to come on a boar hunt. And indeed, pretty much every Greek hero alive at the time went to hunt the boar: **Atalanta** and **Theseus** and **Jason** (of the Argonauts) and Eurytion (also an Argonaut) and Priam (who later fought at Troy) and **Pirithous** and **Amphiaraus** and Peleus (the father of **Achilles**) and Castor and Pollux and so many people I'm not even going to bother boldfacing them. Atalanta, the great huntress who was herself a disciple of Artemis, drew first blood with one of her arrows, and later Meleager himself finished the boar off. It hardly seemed like a fair fight! With this many great heroes together, what kind of monster couldn't they kill?

But nevertheless, the boar got its licks in, and four of the hunters died that day—three from tuskings, and one because Peleus got excited and threw his spear awry, such that it hit not the boar but Eurytion.

(Shortly afterward Meleager got into a fight with some of the hunters over who deserved credit for the kill, and he ended up killing two of them and then dying himself, but maybe that doesn't count.)

> "I prophesy thy death, my living sorrow,
> If thou encounter with the boar tomorrow."
>
> —Shakespeare, *Venus and Adonis* (1593).

"A Wilde Bor"

Bevis of Hampton was an orphaned nobleman from southern England who was sold into slavery and ended up in the court of the

king of Armenia. There he learned that a man-eating "wilde bor" with impervious skin was (as you will note boars do) ravaging the countryside. Bevis being Bevis, he went boar hunting.

His weapons could not pierce the boar's impervious hide, so Bevis (in the words of the old romance):

> "In at the mouth 'gan thrust through
> And carved its heart even a-two"

Which is to say, Bevis stuck his sword straight down the boar's throat and sliced its heart into two pieces.

Somehow, he was able to cut the boar's head off and bring it back to the king as proof, so maybe its impervious skin got weaker after death?

The Boar of Ben Bulben

The deadly Boar of Ben Bulben had no ears or tail, but it did have a pelt filled with poisonous bristles. The pelt was also as invulnerable as a man-eating Armenian boar's. Those deadly nature-boys, the Fianna, once stumbled across the boar's hunting grounds and soon found themselves gored and scattered.

Diarmuid O'Duibhne—the handsomest of the Fianna—struck the boar with his famous sword Begallta, but the blade just snapped in two. Nothing daunted, Diarmuid jumped on the boar's back and bludgeoned it to death with the hilt. Totally successful!

They skinned the boar—but then came the complication. Years before, Diarmuid (so handsome!) had run off with **Finn Mac Cool**'s fiancée, and Finn Mac Cool was the leader of the Fianna. He had a lot of unresolved hostility toward Diarmuid.

"You did a great job killing that enormous boar," Finn said to Diarmuid, with an edge in his voice. "I wonder how big it was."

To determine the size of a boar in an age without tape measures,

Diarmuid was forced to walk along the center of the boar's pelt, counting his paces. Of course, it was a very large boar, even if I don't remember the exact number of paces long—fifteen or seventy-three—and Diarmuid paced the whole thing, snout to tail.

"Interesting," said Finn. "Just to make sure, why don't you pace it again the other way?"

Diarmuid turned around and began to pace. But of course, a boar's bristles run smooth and flat if you rub them one way, like the fur on a dog's back. Rub them the other way . . .

A poisoned bristle immediately lodged in Diarmuid's foot, and the hero collapsed in agony.

"Oops," said Finn Mac Cool, perhaps insincerely.

The boar was actually Diarmuid's half brother, reincarnated into pig form by a druid, but that's too complicated to worry about. Finn Mac Cool had the power to heal Diarmuid by carrying water in his hands from a nearby spring, but that's all beside the story. We're giving advice about killing boars here!

To Review:
What Can We Learn from the Boar Tales?

Gather an enormous army of heroes to hunt boars; always goes great!

The way to a boar's heart is down its gullet.

For Pete's sake, don't walk on boar skins.

Fighting Miscellaneous Monsters

DRAGONS AND GIANTS AND EVEN BOARS ARE FINE THINGS TO FIGHT, BUT naturally the world is filled with all manner of other kinds of monsters to worry about. In Bengal, **Bhima** killed the man-eating demon Bakasura. In Crete, **Theseus** killed the half-man, half-bull Minotaur. In Menling Gongma, high in the Himalayas, **Gesar of Ling** killed a nine-headed tortoise that sported a gem made of lightning embedded in each skull, and an enormous horned lizard with iron eyes and a diamond heart, and a . . . well, Gesar was always off killing something or other, and always something with a complicated description.

Frequently enough, monsters (much like boars and freakish knights) turn out to have impenetrable skin that is impervious to damage from weapons. This ruins the whole point of what weapons are *for*! When **Hercules** fought the impervious Nemean lion, he ended up squeezing it and crushing its bones through its skin. When **Beowulf** found his sword useless against the man-eating Grendel, he ripped the monster's arm off. When **Roland** couldn't harm the sea monster Orc, he crawled down its esophagus and attacked it from inside. And then there's the hideous horned demon Fulad-Zereh who could only be harmed by King Solomon's magical sword Samsir-e Zomorrodnegar . . . so the Egyptian hero **Amir Arsalan** just went and acquired King Solomon's magical sword Samsir-e

Zomorrodnegar before he fought the demon. There's generally a workaround.

But even if they don't have impenetrable skin, they'll probably have teeth or tentacles or who knows what? Laser eyes and poison stings. Every monster or class of monsters requires a different strategy. As always, ideas for how to approach a monster are provided by Apprentice Academy alumni. You'll be amazed how far you can get in life if you just *copy other knights' work*.

Shape-shifters

The most famous contest of a knight against a shape-shifter was when **Menelaus**, king of Sparta, was lost off the coast of Egypt and trying to get the ever-changing sea god Proteus to tell him the way home. Menelaus surprised the shape-shifter and grabbed him in a wrestling hold. In quick succession, Proteus took the form of a lion, a snake, a leopard, a boar (!), a waterfall, and a tree, but Menelaus never relaxed his grasp, so finally Proteus gave up and told Menelaus what he needed to hear.

Don't ask me how to keep a wrestling hold on a waterfall. The point is, it worked. Proteus probably should have become a porcupine, but I'm not the boss of sea gods.

Somewhat deadlier was that shape-shifting dwarf of the Caucasus Mountains, Soseruquo, who used to hunt Narts for sport. He would take the form of an old shoe lying in the street, for example, and then, when a passing Nart went to investigate, turn himself into a thick fog, causing the Nart to stumble around blindly until the fog that was Soseruquo would coalesce behind the Nart's back . . . into a lion or an elephant, or an elephant holding a lion in its trunk, or something else deadly that you wouldn't want to have attacking you in the back. In this way Soseruquo killed Nart after Nart, and always got away with it. The Narts, tough as they were, just gave up hope.

But sometimes—probably usually, but don't tell your teachers this—it is not time for sword swinging and muscle flexing and all the things Narts were good at. Sometimes you have to stop and observe. An old Nartish woman, Saquuna, did just that. And she noticed that Soseruquo, no matter what form he took—lion or elephant or what— always had wobbly thighs. And she counseled the Narts.

The Narts sent word out that they wished to issue a test to Soseruquo: Could he block an iron discus that they threw at him?

Soseruquo, cocky as ever, showed up in his true form, a sinister-looking dwarf. The Narts threw the discus, but Soseruquo just punched it and ricocheted the disk back at them. They barely ducked in time.

"Good, good," said the Narts, again operating off Saquuna's advice. "But now can you do the same thing with your elbows?"

Soseruquo was sure he could, so the Narts gave a throw. Soseruquo whacked the discus with his elbow, and again it came sailing back.

"Sure, but that was easy," the Narts said. This was the final stage of Saquuna's plan. "A true hero," they said, "would be able to bounce it back with his thighs."

Soseruquo assented, but when the Narts threw the discus, and Soseruquo stuck his thighs out—*shhhhk*—his thighs, it turned out, were completely boneless, and the discus went right through them both. Soseruquo collapsed to the ground, and lay there, unable to change shape or escape—but also unable to die from a wound as trifling as the loss of both legs—until a vulture flew down and ate him.

Chimera

The Chimera had three fire-breathing heads—one of a lion, one of a goat, and one of a serpent. This made it particularly challenging to fight: When you were busy fighting one head, the other two would eat you. Also, there was the fire thing.

But the fire proved to be the Chimera's undoing. **Bellerophon**, riding on the winged steed Pegasus, flew over the Chimera, too high

to be in danger. Bellerophon came equipped with a long lance, on the end of which he had attached a blob of lead. From a distance he dangled the lead blob above the Chimera's mouth. Its fiery breath melted the lead, which plunged down the Chimera's gullet. Molten lead in the pipes killed the Chimera.

Of course, the Chimera had three heads, and three mouths. Did Bellerophon repeat the trick twice more? Or did the Chimera only have one stomach, and pouring molten lead down any esophagus was sufficient to kill the beast? Or did B. only manage to kill one head and then fly away, waiting for the necrotic power of one dead body part to slowly kill the rest of the monster? Any way you slice it, the plan worked, and there was no more Chimera.

The Cloud-Eater

The great shaggy beast known as the Cloud-Eater dwelt on a tall mountain in what is now New Mexico, consuming passing clouds. Its voracious appetite ensured that no clouds remained in the sky long, and certainly no rain fell.

Enter the hero **Ahaiyuta**, who had vowed to kill the monster. Fortunately, Ahaiyuta possessed several magic feathers, one of which let him talk to animals and one of which let him shrink to a tiny size for as long as he kept it stuck in his hair.

With one feather, Ahaiyuta befriended a nearby gopher, and persuaded the creature to tunnel its way into the Cloud-Eater's secret cave. The gopher crept up to the sleeping beast and started gnawing away at its fur in the area right over its heart. This woke the Cloud-Eater, naturally, but when it inquired, the gopher just said it was helping out, grooming for nits. The Cloud-Eater went back to sleep.

Ahaiyuta, meanwhile, had shrunk himself small enough that he could crawl through the gopher's tunnel. Popping out, he readied an arrow, and, as the waking Cloud-Eater drew itself upright, aimed at the patch of short hair — right over its heart. No more Cloud-Eater. For a little while, at least, New Mexico got some rain.

Other Skills You Might Want to Master

Hunting

Hunting may seem less imperative now that you can order groceries with your phone, and, indeed, it is no longer taught at the Apprentice Academy. But for years hunting was the preeminent way for knights to hone their skills when not actually in combat with knights or monsters. Many of the techniques are the same: riding a horse really fast, shooting arrows accurately, sticking a spear into a living being. Compared to battling giants, say, hunting may seem a safe bet, but the truth is *hunting is incredibly dangerous. There are boars!*

Despite the danger, many a famous knight has found hunting to be handy practice. For example:

» Digenes Akrites

Digenes Akrites, who later grew to fame fighting bandits and the occasional dragon on the borders of the Persian and Byzantine empires, learned to fight by hunting. At the age of twelve he could kill deer and even bears with his bare hands. He also hunted lions, but for lions he brought a sword. No need for foolish risks!

Some years later, Digenes Akrites was hunting with the Byzantine emperor Basil when a lion attacked the emperor. Digenes was unarmed—he'd been hunting deer after all—but he was now old enough and practiced enough that he managed to grab the lion by a hind leg, whirl its body around, and dash it dead against the ground.

Some years after that, the emperor Basil went hunting without Digenes Akrites, and his belt got tangled in the horns of a stag, who dragged him for eighteen miles, and that was the end of the emperor Basil. *Hunting is really dangerous!*

» Yamato Takeru

As if animals weren't bad enough, hunting also involves *other people*, and, sad to say, some people just cannot be trusted.

Yamato Takeru was once out hunting with some rivals, and they set alight the tall, dry grass all around. Surely the fire would destroy him!

Yamato, though, had his sword Kusanagi no Tsurugi, which had been pulled from a serpent's tail by the storm god. When he perceived the danger he was in, Yamato Takeru started swinging that sword, chopping grass until he found himself in a safe area, with no tall grass near him to burn. Then he just had to wait until the fire burned itself out.

This is how the sword got the name Kusanagi no Tsurugi, which means "grass cutter."

I tell this tale to drive home the point that fancy magic swords are useful for more than just stabbing monsters and things. There's also yardwork.

A Maxim of the Fianna: So long as thou shalt live, thy lord forsake not; neither for gold nor for other reward in the world abandon one whom thou art pledged to protect.

» Osla Gyllellfawr

And some people even try to hunt boars? **Osla Gyllellfawr** was out boar hunting when his knife accidentally fell out of its sheath and was lost. As the boar ran across a river, Osla, in pursuit, found that the knife had been so big, the sheath so capacious, that the empty sheath filled up with water and the weight dragged Osla down into the deeps, where he drowned.

Try to restrict yourself to hunting safer things, like lions.

"The wild boar of Japan is a most ferocious beast, with gaping jaws well furnished with sharp teeth and long white tusks, and woe to him who falls a prey to the animal."

—Buto, "Boar Hunting in Japan," *The Japan Magazine* (1914)

Archery

Acquiring or faking skill at archery can be important, no mistake. **Odysseus** shot an arrow through the eyes of twelve lined-up ax heads, and his rivals were so stunned that they just stood there slack-jawed while he aimed his next several arrows at them. There's also the fact that Archery 101 is a big part of your freshman year GPA at Apprentice Academy. This is no problem, assuming you're really good at archery! But life is, as always, hard for the rest of us.

The Lakota hero **Iktomi**—some people say he's a spider and some people say he's a reprobate, but I don't believe such slanders—once came across a local boy who was heading off to woo a chieftain's daughter, looking to impress everybody with his bow-and-arrow skills.

"If you're so good at shooting, let's see you put an arrow in the top of this tree," said Iktomi. And the local boy complied.

"Are you sure that arrow struck true?" Iktomi said. "I can't see it." So the local boy clambered up the tree to pluck the arrow out. On his way down, he found himself climbing through a lasso, and next thing he knew he was bound to the tree trunk with rope—Iktomi had been waiting for him. And Iktomi picked up the bow and arrow and went off to meet the chieftain's daughter.

"You may have heard of that nearby guy who was really good at archery?" Iktomi told everyone. "Well, that's me!"

Unfortunately, his story wasn't very persuasive, and his rope wasn't very strong, and soon Iktomi got caught out. But his theory was sound. The only question is *how do you fake skill at archery more convincingly than Iktomi did?*

The most famous trick for becoming a great archer is to practice shooting your arrows at a wall. After the arrow hits, wherever it hits, draw a bull's-eye around it. In this way you will always have hit the bull's-eye, by definition.

Robin Hood's signature move was to wait for someone to shoot a bull's-eye and then shoot his arrow such that it split the shaft of his opponent's arrow from fletching to point. I've tried splitting one arrow with another by holding both in my hands and hammering them together, and I could never get it to work even at that simpler level. You might be able to saw an arrow halfway down, though, stick another arrow into the split, and then shoot both arrows together at a wall. The force of impact would then drive the rear arrow forward, completing the split. At that point you can run forward and draw a bull's-eye around the arrows. Do it quick and when no one is looking.

"The guy with the first arrow just left town," you explain. "He said he had someplace to be. Probably he was just super embarrassed that I split his arrow like that."

Iktomi's rival—how good could he have been, as no one even remembers his name?—was skilled at the traditional Lakota archery contests of bringing down hares as they darted past and piercing leaves as they tumbled from trees. Your classmates will probably be busy spending their time practicing the former (it's just about the least dangerous kind of hunting), so you might want to get really good at the latter, and then, whenever an archery contest is proposed, insist that shooting leaves is the ultimate test of skill. Shooting leaves is a great leveler, because no one's very good at it; leaves tend to fall in crazy, unpredictable patterns, and the only way to hit them is blind luck, the sole resource a skilled and unskilled archer have equal reserves of.

A little observation will show you, though, that the way leaves fall is not completely crazy nor completely unpredictable. There's a method to their madness, as the Danish prince **Amleth** (House Pismire, class of 867) might say. Longer, narrower leaves *flutter*, moving back and forth like a rocking cradle as they fall, while shorter, rounder leaves tend to *tumble*, somersaulting end over end on their way down. Scope out the general shape of leaves on a nearby tree, and you'll be halfway to predicting their motions. After that, it's up to luck or skill, whichever you've got.

Hairbreadth escapes

Knights get captured by giants, other knights, and sorcerers, and that's just the way it is. In general, escape is not too hard. Giants' manacles are rarely sized for human wrists; other knights are only interested in *taking* prisoners, and never pay attention to *keeping* prisoners; and as for sorcerers—they tend to turn you into a statue or a tree, so you have several centuries to come up with a plan for escape. When in doubt, bribe the fellow who brings you your food bucket. It's not a high-paying job.

More exotic methods of imprisonment, though, call for different methods of escape. Your Apprentice Academy instructors are loath to advise you on how to work an escape, because they are afraid you will use the knowledge to get out of detention. But I (as always!) am here to help . . .

» Escaping from donkey's skin

The trap: **Shapur Z'ul Aktaf**, emperor of Persia, disguised himself as a merchant and traveled incognito to Constantinople, to see if he could learn whether the Byzantine emperor there was a good and just man. Turns out the Byzantine emperor was not. What was worse, someone tipped the Byzantine emperor off, and he decided to seize Shapur as a spy. To prevent Shapur from escaping the imperial prison, the Byzantine developed an unusually humiliating set of chains: He sewed Shapur up in the skin of a donkey. When the skin dried, it held Shapur in place as tightly as a straitjacket.

The escape: Shapur requested some warm milk be brought to him at mealtime to accompany the bread and water he usually received. Shapur didn't drink the milk, however: He rubbed it into the donkey's skin, until it started to soften. After two weeks, Shapur was able to wriggle out of the pliant skin and effect his escape.

(Make sure you bring milk along with you.)

» Escaping from a man-eating wolf

The trap: **Sigmund** and his nine brothers were captured by the wicked King Siggeir of the Geats. The king placed the brothers in stocks—their hands and feet immobilized—in the middle of the woods. Every night at midnight, an ancient she-wolf would come out of the woods and eat one of the brothers while he writhed helplessly in the stocks. Then she would amble off deeper into the forest while the remaining brothers waited all through the day. At midnight she would come again . . .

The escape: For nine nights the she-wolf ate her fill, until there was only Sigmund left in the stocks. On the tenth night, Queen Signy of the Geats—who happened to be Sigmund's twin sister—came and smeared honey on Sigmund's face. When the she-wolf started licking the honey off Sigmund's face (as an appetizer), Sigmund grabbed her tongue in his teeth. The alarmed she-wolf thrashed around until she had shattered the stocks, but Sigmund would still not let go. Finally, the tongue tore out at the root, and the wolf bled to death, whereupon Sigmund slipped away to plot his vengeance on King Siggeir.

(Make sure you bring honey along with you.)

» Escaping from a trapped bed

The trap: Once, when **Sir Lancelot** was questing to rescue a kidnapped Queen Guinevere (as was the custom of the time), he took shelter in a tower where he was offered dinner and a bed for the night. In the same room as his own bed was another, much nicer bed, its mattress stuffed with feathers and its coverlet trimmed with finest sable. Lancelot was warned that the fancy bed was too dangerous to sleep in, but warning Lancelot of danger was like waving a red flag in front of a bull, or a Red Bull in front of a med student. Lancelot put on his pajamas

and hopped into the deadly bed, but at midnight . . . *a flaming lance* shot out of the ceiling right at him!

The escape: Trapped beds — usually called "perilous beds" — were surprisingly common in the days of King Arthur, so it's important for a serious knight to be ready for them. Lancelot cunningly slept not in the middle, but on one side of the bed, so the lance didn't transfix him, but merely grazed his side. The slight nick woke him up, however, so although the flame from the lance set the bed on fire, Lancelot was able to put it out before going back to sleep, there on that same smoldering bed.

(Make sure you bring an extra pillow along with you.)

≫ Escaping from a house on fire

The trap: Sometimes people set your house on fire. What do you want from me?

The escape: When **Skarphedinn** found himself trapped in a burning building with his family and no way out, he took Ogress of War, his famous ax, and buried its blade in a gable wall of the house. In this way, when the fire raged around and killed him, the blade of the ax remained pristine and sharp — all the better for someone to avenge the whole family with it.

Contrarily, when **Sesostris** found himself trapped in a burning building with his family and no way out, he took two of his children, tossed their bodies on the flames, and used their corpses as a bridge to dash outside.

Now, I'm not telling you what to do, but it's probably a good idea to walk around occasionally announcing, "By gum, I sure am more of a Scarphedinn than a Sesostris," especially in front of any children you have, so that if a fire ever hits, they won't be expecting your next move.

(Make sure you bring your kids along with you.)

70

Seeing in the dark

If you come upon an opponent in a cave or a darkened forest, try this trick **Dietrich of Bern** used when he met the giant Ecke on a moonless night. Dietrich simply banged his sword against some rocks and sized the giant up by the glow of the sparks that shot out. They immediately joined combat, Dietrich and the giant, and from that point on, the area was illuminated by the sparks of their clashing swords.

A word of caution, though. Too many sparks can cause a fire. In the days of Charlemagne, two knights, **Pinabel** and **Thierry**, were dueling when one of Pinabel's blows struck sparks off Thierry's helmet. The sparks set fire to the dry grass around their feet, and the duel would have been delayed if with his very next blow Thierry had not cloven Pinabel's skull in two. After that, Thierry was able to put out the fire at his leisure.

It may be easiest just to get some kind of magical item, though. The best knight in the French court—**Roland**, and then, two hundred years later, **Raoul de Cambrai**—used to wear a special helmet with a nosepiece of gold and a gem set in the front that could light up, casting a guiding light, like a coal miner's hardhat.

Actually, probably easier to obtain than an ancient French magic item would be a coal miner's hardhat.

The bluff

It is well known (among Apprentice Academy students) that if you can get your harried instructors to assume your work is always excellent, they'll give your paper an A without even glancing at whatever nonsense you scrawled out. Similarly, if everyone assumes you're going to defeat them, you never have to fight.

The great beast Iya, whose very breath could suck the life from a body, leaving a shriveled husk-corpse behind, roamed the shores of the Great Lakes, straight-up murdering the locals, until one evening the always reliable Lakota hero **Iktomi** decided to do something about

it. Iktomi sent a magpie ahead of him to bring news to Iya—that the great Iktomi was coming, that he was dreadfully angry at Iya, that in fact he was so angry he had grabbed the moon and broken off a big piece to use as a bow.

Iya quickly glanced up at the evening moon, which, indeed, was missing a bow-shaped chunk. It was a three quarter moon, so this was hardly surprising, but perhaps Iya was usually too busy murdering people to waste much time in moon gazing.

And then Iya saw—here came Iktomi, and he was carrying something. As Iya watched, Iktomi took the bow in his hand and bent it . . . until it matched the curve of the moon's missing chunk.

That was enough for Iya, who turned his massive frame and began to run away.

But of course, Iya's danger lay in his deadly breath. With his back turned, Iktomi could run right up behind him, and—well, perhaps Iktomi was not the greatest of archers, but Iya was as wide as the broad side of a barn, a size proverbially difficult to miss.

It took a lot of arrows, but Iktomi got him in the end. So to speak.

Sometimes you don't have to sound invincible—you just have to make fighting you sound like it's not worth it.

Alexander the Great, king of Macedon, when fighting against the country of Zang, gave his army legs of mutton to eat as the enemy spied on them. "This human flesh sure does taste good!" Alexander's soldiers said loudly, and the terrified spies ran back to report that an entire army of cannibals had come into the kingdom. Zang surrendered not long after. Who wants to fight and risk getting eaten by Macedonians?

Stalling

One of the all-time great techniques is the stall, mastered by **Oishi**

Kuranosuke, leader of the famous Forty-Seven Ronin. Oishi's feudal lord had been unjustly executed thanks to the machinations of a courtier named Kira. Oishi got forty-six of his fellow samurai to agree to avenge their lord's death by killing Kira.

The problem was, of course, that Kira was expecting it. Everyone was expecting it. Everyone was ready for an attack, which is the worst time to make an attack, generally. Forty-seven ronin—a ronin is just a samurai without a master, in this case because the master was executed and therefore dead—were no match for the forces an influential fellow like Kira could muster to guard him.

So the forty-seven ronin did . . . nothing.

Some became grifters and some became hoboes, and Oishi Kuranosuke was the worst of all, a drunken dissolute lout that passersby would spit on in the street. "These losers are not samurai," people said, "especially that sad little bottom-feeder, Oishi."

Kira's spies heard this, of course, for they heard almost everything. And Kira began to relax. The only people with a grudge against him were in no position to do anything but wallow in their own intemperance. Doubtless, he was safe.

For two years or thereabouts this went on, until Kira's contempt for the sad, slovenly Forty-Seven Ronin was so deeply felt that his guardsmen stopped guarding and his watchmen stopped watching.

And of course that's when Oishi gathered his forty-six companions and struck. They stormed Kira's compound from both sides, rooted out the malefactor, and cut off his head. Then they turned themselves in to the authorities, which is a very House Martlet thing to do, and is, I stress, optional. The key is the stalling, without which none of this would have worked.

I myself am involved in several very long stalls, seeking to lull ancient enemies into false senses of complacency. Several of these enemies have died natural deaths while I stalled, which is probably for the best. Still waiting on others, but in the meantime, this dissolute lifestyle I'm faking isn't going to live itself!

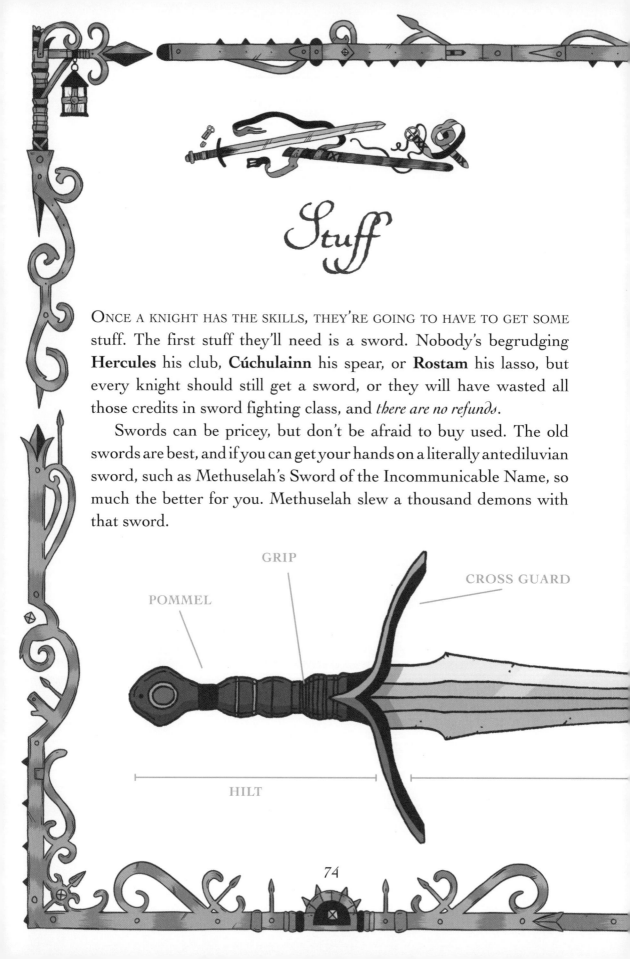

Stuff

Once a knight has the skills, they're going to have to get some stuff. The first stuff they'll need is a sword. Nobody's begrudging **Hercules** his club, **Cúchulainn** his spear, or **Rostam** his lasso, but every knight should still get a sword, or they will have wasted all those credits in sword fighting class, and *there are no refunds*.

Swords can be pricey, but don't be afraid to buy used. The old swords are best, and if you can get your hands on a literally antediluvian sword, such as Methuselah's Sword of the Incommunicable Name, so much the better for you. Methuselah slew a thousand demons with that sword.

GRIP

CROSS GUARD

POMMEL

HILT

A good sword has more than one owner. The wondrous Dragvandil ("no sword was there more biting," the saga says) was first owned by Kettle Hæing, who gave it to his son Grim Shaggy-skin, who gave it to Thorolf Kveldulfsson, who gave it to his brother Skallagrim, who gave it to his son Thorolf, who gave it to Arinbjorn, who gave it to Thorolf's brother **Egil Skallgrimsson**. Charlemagne, upon his death, bequeathed his personal sword Joyeuse to his young champion, **Guillaume d'Orange**. Or: The bronze sword Flamberge, which had been worn by the traitorous Antenor back in the Trojan War, ended up by the seventh century in the hands of **Begon de Belin**, who wielded it in the internecine feuds between his houses of Lorraine and Bordeaux—so puissant was Begon with this blade that even when he stood alone and the Bordelais surrounded him, he held them all off until finally they shot him down from a distance with arrows—before being passed on to its most famous owner, **Renaud de Montauban**, and then, a generation later, to **Galien le Restoré**, son of the Paladin **Oliver**, who used it to avenge his father's death.

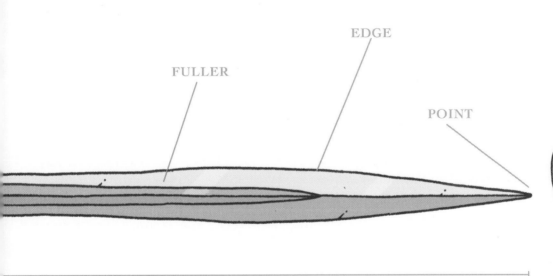

EDGE

FULLER

POINT

BLADE

Other Famous Swords and Their Owners

Sword	Knight
Almace	Turpin
Arondight	Lancelot
Azoth	Paracelsus
Begallta	Diarmuid
Belisarda	Roger
Corchense	Ban of Benwick (Lancelot's father)
Cortana	Ogier the Dane
Crocea Mors	Julius Caesar
Cruaidín Catutchenn	Cúchulainn
Eckesachs	Dietrich of Bern (after he gave Nagelring to Heime)
Galatine	Gawain
Hauteclere	Oliver
Honjo Masamune	Honjo Shigenaga
Hrunting	Unferth (Beowulf borrows it)
Izuminokami Fujiwara Kaneshige	Miyamoto Musashi
Lagulf	Hildebrand
Laufi	Bödvar Bjarki
Merveilleuse	Doon of Mayence (grandfather of Ogier and Renaud)
Mistletoe	Hrómundr Gripsson
Morgelai	Bevis
Murgleis	Ganelon
Nagelring	Heime (after Dietrich was done with it)
Nistrimsha	Pradyumna
Philippan	Mark Antony
Quern-biter	Haakon the Good
Ridill	Regin
Rose	Ortnit
Samsir-e Zomorrodnegar	Amir Arsalan
Sauvagine	Ogier (he had two)

Sometimes getting a fancy sword is easy. A hand came out of a lake holding Excalibur and three minutes later **King Arthur** was buckling it on his belt. **Witege**'s father was Wayland, the legendary smith, so presumably his dad just made Mimung and handed it over to him. But not everyone is going to be so lucky. If you can't afford a great, or even magical, sword, and if you aren't on Wayland's Christmas list — well, some people might suggest you could steal a sword. But stealing is wrong! I would never counsel stealing! Instead, I would suggest trying one of these six methods: blackmailing, welching, finding, plundering, stabbing, or grave robbing.

Blackmailing: Tyrfing

Svafrlami, while riding alone just before dawn, came upon two dwarves who were hurrying to return to their underground lair before the rays of the sun could turn them to stone (as was the custom with certain dwarves). Svafrlami barred their path and refused to let the dwarves reach safety until they had agreed to forge him the wonderfullest of all swords.

Now, even great human smiths such as Ilmarinen or Wayland have a hard time matching the magic of a dwarven forge. So when the dwarves agreed to deliver a sword in a month's time, Svafrlami knew he had made a splendid bargain. Tyrfing shone like the sun when it was drawn from the scabbard, and no sword had a sharper edge.

The downside: Perhaps the dwarves were less pleased than Svafrlami with the way things had transpired. After the month had passed, after they had handed the promised sword over, after they had already begun slipping back into the tunnel to their underground kingdom, one of the dwarves happened to mention — a remark he casually tossed over his shoulder, like salt — that the sword was totally cursed, that every time it was drawn it would kill a man, that the sword would perform three evil deeds, and that it would be the death of Svafrlami . . . which wasn't even one of the three evil deeds, because Svafrlami completely deserved it!

Indeed, when Svafrlami was dueling the Viking Arngrim, he whiffed with Tyrfing, and the sword—so sharp it was!—sliced into the earth, where it embedded itself deep, and stuck. Svafrlami was still trying to pull it free when Arngrim chopped off his hand. Then, at his leisure, Arngrim drew Tyrfing from the ground and with it slew Svafrlami.

And that wasn't even one of the three evil deeds! Arngrim gave the sword to his berserker son **Angantyr**, but he and his eleven berserk brothers died fighting **Hjalmar** and **Kormak**—Kormak alone survived that encounter, and he thought the sword too cursed to bring with him. He had it buried with Angantyr. And there its evil should have stayed . . . but Angantyr had an infant daughter, and when she grew up, she wanted that sword. Her name was **Hervarth**, and she had joined a Viking pirate crew, working her way up the ranks until she was their commander. If only she had an evil sword, her life would be complete!

So Hervarth made her crew sail to the haunted island of Samsø, where her father and his sword were buried. The other Vikings were too scared to land, but Hervarth got into a little skiff alone and rowed herself to shore. By day she walked among the barrows—the mounds beneath which the dead were buried—and at night she noted which barrow glowed with an unearthly blue light. That's the one she wanted!

Hervarth approached the barrow and called out to the ghost of her father, demanding the blade that was her birthright. The barrow cracked open, and the moldering corpse of Angantyr, his flesh still gashed and split from the blows he'd received at Hjalmar's hand the day Tyrfing failed him, emerged.

"My only child," he said to Hervarth in a sad, hollow voice, "you do not want this terrible sword."

But Hervarth did. There is not much one can threaten the dead with, perhaps, the worst already having happened to them, by definition. But corpses do prefer to be comfortable, and Hervarth threatened to

bring ants—an entire ant colony—to Angantyr's barrow, into which the ants would burrow, thereupon to crawl forever on his corpse, itching him with their tiny feet . . . if he did not hand over Tyrfing.

And so he did. And Tyrfing was back in the world.

The dwarf wasn't joking when he'd said any time the sword was drawn it had to kill somebody. One of Hervarth's sons was showing his brother Tyrfing; he drew the sword to display its beautiful blade, but when he sought to put it back in its scabbard, the sword jumped in his hand and slew his brother. It would not be sheathed until it had drunk blood.

(That was one of the three evil deeds, but of course there were two more!)

Yes, this is a really long *downside*, but that's Tyrfing for you!

Welching: The Sword of Seven Waters

The Estonian hero **Kalevipoeg** traveled to Finland to bargain with the first smith, Ilmarinen, that he might forge him a sword. The price they agreed to was immense—nine draft horses, eight packhorses, twenty oxen, fifty calves, large cargos of wheat, barley, and rye, several hundred items of jewelry, a thousand dollars cash, one third of a kingdom, and three princesses' dowries—but it was worth it, such was the sword Ilmarinen forged for Kalevipoeg—the Sword of Seven Waters, which had a will of its own and could talk.

Of course, Kalevipoeg wasn't going to be able to pay. Regardless, as an alumnus of House Biscione in good standing, Kalevipoeg started boasting, at a celebratory dinner with Ilmarinen's family, about his past exploits, until Ilmarinen's son blew him an incredulous raspberry. One thing led to another; there was a fight in the dining room, Kalevipoeg killed Ilmarinen's son with his new sword, and he ran off into the night. No payment required.

(If you wanted to try Kalevipoeg's welching method, you could always skip the part where you murder the guy, and just book it.)

The downside: As Kalevipoeg fled, Ilmarinen called out for vengeance

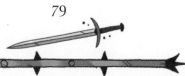

to the only sentient being that might be able to help him—the Sword of Seven Waters.

It happened that, some time later, a sorcerer stole the sword from a sleeping Kalevipoeg, but the sword wriggled like a thing possessed, and slipped from the sorcerer's grasp as he was flying over the stream Käpä. The weapon sank into the water.

When Kalevipoeg woke he went looking for the sword, calling to it like a dog. The sword answered and said it was somewhere at the bottom of the Käpä.

"Well, come back to me," Kalevipoeg said.

The sword, though, reminded Kalevipoeg that he was a scummy murderer, and refused to budge.

"Fine," sighed Kalevipoeg. "Just promise me this: If whoever brought you here comes to cross the river, you'll take the opportunity to cut both his legs off." Kalevipoeg was referring to the sorcerer, but perhaps there was an ambiguity to his words.

A Maxim of the Fianna: Stand not up to take part in a brawl.

"I'll remember what you said," answered the sword.

And some time after that, Kalevipoeg was wandering around and happened to ford the Käpä without really noticing what stream it was. But of course he figured it out when the Sword of Seven Waters came zipping downstream and chopped off both of his legs. That was the end of Kalevipoeg.

Finding: The whip sword

Sayf Ben Dhi Yazan was recruited by a hunchbacked, beetle-browed sorcerer named 'Abd Lahab who shot sparks out of his eyes. This 'Abd Lahab had discovered in some ancient manuscripts the location of a forbidden treasure cave, here in the Ethiopian highlands. While he chanted spells to keep the cave open, why couldn't Sayf Ben Dhi Yazan slip in and grab the treasure?

80

So the two traveled to a certain place, and as 'Abd Lahab began his incantations, lo, a hole opened in the ground. Sayf Ben Dhi Yazan entered, and the first thing he found, lying on a gilded ivory pedestal, was a whip. As he lifted it, it snapped forward, and the whip was in fact a sword, a flexible sword that could coil like rope; but when a skillful wielder cracked it, the whip sword could slice through rock. Maybe Sayf Ben Dhi Yazan tried it out on the ivory pedestal. Soon he was climbing painstakingly out of the hole. Easy as pie.

The downside: Of course, of course 'Abd Lahab said with an innocent whistle, "It'll be easier to climb out if you hand me the whip sword." And of course, Sayf Ben Dhi Yazan ended up having to snap that whip, whipping the head off the sorcerer. Sayf Ben Dhi Yazan had never had a good time with sorcerers—his mother was one, and she'd dumped him in the African wilderness to die. At least killing 'Abd Lahab must have been less traumatic than all the terrible adventures Sayf Ben Dhi Yazan had with his mother.

Anyway, the *Aladdin Principle* (as they call it) is that if someone sends you into a forbidden treasure cave, *watch out*. Sayf Ben Dhi Yazan was lucky he remembered the Aladdin Principle in time.

Plundering: Durendal

Hector fought with Durendal in the Trojan War, but **Achilles**, after he'd slain Hector, plundered the sword from his corpse. In pity, Achilles returned Durendal to the Trojans, along with Hector's body, for burial, but one of those things was too good to bury, and the Trojans passed the sword to their Amazon ally, Queen **Penthesilea**. Achilles once again faced Durendal when he met Penthesilea in single combat, but he slew her, too, and took back Durendal.

Soon Achilles's 95% invulnerability betrayed him, and he fell on the Plains of Troy as well, and in the ensuing chaos, Durendal was lost for over a thousand years. By the eighth century it ended up in the hands of a Saracen named **Aumon**, who brought it with him when he invaded France. A young **Roland** beat Aumon—in single combat again—and plundered from Aumon's corpse not only Durendal, but also Aumon's horse Brigliador, which he renamed Veillantif, and his Oliphant—a horn made from an elephant's tusk.

The downside: What one plunders may be plundered in turn. When Roland was mortally wounded at the battle of Roncevaux, he desperately tried to shatter Durendal against the rocks, so that no one could take his precious sword, as he had taken it from Aumon. But no mere stone is hard enough to shatter Durendal, and Roland just ended up cleaving a bunch of rocks until he gave up and died.

Stabbing: The Kris of Pu Gandring

Ken Angrok was a foundling who had been raised on the island of Java by a professional thief named Lembong. Ken Angrok was a knight at heart, though, and soon swore off thieving—of course a few semesters at the Apprentice Academy helped! After graduation, Ken Angrok decided his true destiny would be to assassinate the king of East Java and marry his wife, Dedes.

The king of East Java was, however, immune to all existing weapons, and Ken Angrok would need a new one to take him out. He went to the great smith Pu Gandring and asked him to make a kris—a short sword with a wavy blade—capable of killing the king.

"That'll take twelve months," said Pu Gandring.

"Sure, whatever, I'll be back in five," said Ken Angrok.

Five months later, Ken Angrok returned and demanded the kris.

"You can't have it, as I'm still polishing it," said Pu Gandring.

So, Ken Angrok snatched the kris and stabbed the smith. The kris was almost done anyway.

The downside: With his dying breath, Pu Gandring tried to explain that the kris was unfinished because he had not yet taken the vital step of *rendering it not evil.* He prophesied that the kris would kill seven kings including Ken Angrok himself and his grandchild.

With that, Pu Gandring gave up the ghost. "Sure, whatever," said Ken Angrok. He was already plotting his next move.

First, he loaned the kris to a friend of his, Kebo Hijo, who wore it around proudly and publicly. Then Angrok stole the kris back from that friend and used it to kill the king. When people found the kris sticking in the dead king's heart, they all said, "I've seen that kris before. I remember who had it! It was Kebo Hijo who killed the king!"

While Kebo Hijo went to the axman, Ken Angrok cozied up to Queen Dedes. Soon they were married, and Ken Angrok was now king. He wore the kris.

But Dedes's son from a previous marriage suspected the truth. He asked to have a look at the kris that his stepfather always carried with him. No sooner was the kris in his hands than the youth stabbed Ken Angrok. Pu Gandring's prophecy came true . . . and kept coming true until five more kings were dead.

Grave robbing: Skofnung

Skofnung was King **Hrolf Kraki**'s sword, and it was known as the greatest sword in northern Europe at the time. After the king's death, he was buried with it in Denmark, but after three hundred years an Icelander named Skeggi dug up the grave, grabbed the sword, and passed it down to his son, and so on to friends and sons for several generations until Gellir Thorkelsson reburied it in Denmark.

The downside: You mean other than Samsø-style ghosts? Well, it depends on what kind of sword you get. It turns out that the reason Gellir Thorkelsson decided to return the sword was that it was just too much effort to maintain.

The effort came from the fact that Skofnung's power lay in a tiny magical worm that lived in its pommel. The worm hated sunlight, and so sunlight must never be permitted to land on its pommel house. The worm liked being kept apprised of any upcoming combats, so before every fight Skofnung's owner had to blow on the pommel, the better to draw the worm out, and wait a few minutes while the worm slowly inched into the open (shade it from the sun, please!) and looked around. The worm would prefer that the sword be rotated as it crawled so that it was always right side up, and the crawling was easier. All in all, a difficult little worm!

What happened when someone refused to flatter the whims of the Skofnung worm can be seen in the experiences of the warrior-poet **Kormak**. Kormak was scheduled to duel a man named Bersi, who possessed the famous sword Whitting. Kormak borrowed Skofnung from Skeggi just so he could have a weapon better than Bersi's. But Kormak didn't bother to shield Skofnung's pommel from sunlight, nor did he bother to angle the sword to make crawling easier for the worm. And right away the worm got its revenge. It made the sword stick in its scabbard, so Kormak couldn't draw it until he lay down on the ground with the scabbard in his hand and pushed against the cross guard with his feet. Finally, the sword squeaked free.

And then things got worse. The duel was only to first blood, and when Kormak and Bersi crashed their swords against each other, Skofnung shattered Whitting, such that a fragment of Whitting flew forward and sliced Kormak's hand. Whitting had drawn first blood. Bersi was the winner of the duel.

Perhaps Kormak should have buttered up that worm. But buttering up a worm can grow wearying. If I were Gellir Thorkelsson, I would have kept an early bird around, just to put fear into that uncooperative worm's heart.

"Up, sword, and know thou a more horrid hent."

—Amleth

Messing with other people's swords

Amleth, prince of Denmark, knew that his wicked uncle Feng wanted to kill him; the prince had only managed to stay alive this long by pretending to be a fool. One day he kept drawing his sword in crowded areas and almost sticking people with it (as fools might do) until worried townsfolk got a blacksmith to rivet a nail through

the sword and scabbard, such that he could no longer draw it. Then Amleth snuck into his uncle's bedroom and hung the sword on his bedstead.

At night, when Feng's villainous retainers were all asleep in the big hall, Amleth cut down a large tapestry, let it drift down atop the sleeping men, and staked the tapestry to the ground along its edges. Then he set the great hall on fire. Whatever retainers managed to wriggle free of the staked tapestry and the burning building quickly ran to wake Feng, who figured out the whole catastrophe was the work of his nephew. Grabbing the nearest sword—the one from the bedstead, the one riveted into its scabbard—Feng ran outside looking for said nephew. Who was, of course waiting for him with a new sword.

"Now we'll fight it out," said Feng, who was a great swordsman.

"Suits me," said Amleth, who was House Pismire.

"Then draw!" said Feng. And one of them drew.

That was the end of Feng. This is a good trick, and you should have seen the look on Feng's face!

In a similar vein, **Yamato Takeru**, whose legendary sword Kusanagi no Tsurugi was revered throughout Japan, had a cunning copy of the sword made, with a blade of wood. He walked around with a wooden copy—but since he kept it sheathed, everyone thought it really was Kusanagi—and that *everyone* included the dangerous ruler of rival Izumo province. Yamato suggested to the Izumite that they switch swords and have a friendly duel, and the Izumite, excited to get his hands on Kusanagi even for a playful practice, agreed. They dutifully switched swords, and it was time to draw. Yamato drew a regular sword, a mediocre sword, perhaps, but still a real sword. The Izumite drew a shaft of cheap wood.

A Maxim of the Fianna: Have naught to do with a madman or a wicked one.

"Rats," said the Izumite.

Soon, Izumo province had no ruler.

With less time to prepare (than Amleth or Yamato), **Dietrich of Bern** used a simpler stratagem when he realized he was going to have to fight **Witege**, owner of dread Mimung. Dietrich wielded the great sword Naglering, but Mimung was the deadliest weapon in southern Europe. So Dietrich had his aged friend Hildebrand sneak Mimung from Witege's scabbard when Witege wasn't paying attention, replacing it with some jive second-class sucker sword. Dietrich, meanwhile, had his wonderful sword and magic armor to boot.

(Of course, Dietrich acted like such an obnoxious jerk about the situation that Hildebrand felt bad for Witege, and partway through the fight returned Mimung to him, whereupon things went *very differently*. There's probably a lesson here, but I can't quite figure out what it is.)

One additional suggestion

Back in the fifteenth century, the Swabian master of arms **Hans Talhoffer** used to turn his sword around, grasp the blade, and hit his opponents with the cross guard like a hammer. I'm not sure if fifteenth-century Swabian swords weren't very sharp or if fifteenth-century Swabian gloves were just really thick, but it worked for him . . . note his title *master of arms*.

I imagine the great thing about this technique, if you can pull it off, is how demoralizing it must be for your opponent. While you hit them, you can shout, "Just wait till I turn this sword *around*."

Shields

You're learning to fight using Apprentice Academy equipment, which means for reasons of economy your shields double as billboards, decorated with company logos, in an attempt to drive up advertising revenue. Pity the poor apprentice who has to fight with a shield decorated with the logo of Target.

But someday you'll be out of the academy, and unless you get really famous really fast, you won't be able to rent your shield as ad space. You'll have to find something on your own to put on it.

Decorating shields is an old tradition, and, indeed, different-colored shields can help identify knights from a distance. **Gawain** had his famous shield with a pentagram thereon; King Arthur bore a shield named Pridwen, featuring a likeness of the Virgin Mary; **Sir Galahad's** shield was all white with a red cross painted on it in blood. But the custom is much older than Arthurian times. Achilles bore a shield so intricately carved that describing it took Homer 130 lines in the *Iliad*.

In the eleventh century BC, seven warriors teamed up to unsuccessfully conquer the city of Thebes. Thebes had seven gates, see, and each warrior was supposed to attack one gate and . . . well, you get the picture. But the point was that each hero had his own shield with his own device on it, and by great good fortune, descriptions of those devices have been passed down through the ages to serve as inspiration.

"Lift like flame of Death thy shield,
And thy sword like meteor wield.
Cut down thy foe!"

—Harvey, *Ossian's Fingal* (1814)

The Shields of the
Seven Against Thebes

Knight	The Design
Hippomedon	Fire-breathing snake-man
Tydeus	Full moon surrounded by stars
Capaneus	Man wielding torch above the motto "I'll burn down the town."
Eteoclus	Man climbing siege ladder with the motto "Not even gods can knock me down."
Amphion	A sphinx (the traditional enemy of Thebes)
Amphiaraus	His design was to have no design
Polynices	A woman saying "I am Justice, who shall give him the city."

The Seven Against Thebes (so-called) did not get through the seven gates. Theban heroes repulsed the attackers, and all seven of them died, except possibly **Amphiaraus**, who fell into a crack in the earth while he was running away. Maybe he fell into a magical subterranean land filled with diamond-eyed gnomes; you don't know. Or maybe he plummeted to his death.

Anyway, the point is that all these shield devices are up for grabs now, so take what you will.

Armor

What kind of armor will you want to get? Ask any knight, and they'll quickly answer "magical armor," which, sure, if you can get it.

But a word of caution about magical armor: It's dangerous to over-rely on its protection.

Ortnit (nephew of **Ilya Muromets**) possessed a magical suit of armor that had once belonged to **Dietrich of Bern** some five centuries prior (or, some say, one century later—these records are contradictory). The armor had been hardened in dragon's blood and was impervious to all weapons. Ortnit wore the armor when he went out dragon hunting. Perhaps it made him cocky. Anyway, in a land infested with dragons, he lay down to sleep, armor still on.

And indeed, when a dragon came upon him sleeping and swallowed him whole, the armor protected Ortnit. But then the dragon vomited him back up again, mama-bird style, before her young, and the small dragons with their long tongues sucked Ortnit's flesh through the gaps in the armor's joints, until there was no Ortnit left inside the armor at all.

On the other hand, regular armor is really heavy, and sweaty, and hard to put on, so get magical armor if you possibly can.

Animal Companions

Horses

"It is the prince of palfreys; his neigh is like the bidding of a monarch and his countenance enforces homage."

—Shakespeare, *Henry V* (ca. 1599)

A KNIGHT LIVES AND DIES BY THEIR HORSE. MAYBE SOME GRADUATES OF the Apprentice Academy's knights discipline can go around on foot, or swinging through the trees, but the preferred method is horseback, and a good horse is worth its weight in . . . not *gold*, probably, but something else a little less valuable.

Pegasus can fly and Chal Kuiruk can talk, and **Dietrich of Bern**'s horse Falke once stomped on a giant's back, killing him, when said giant was busy pinning Dietrich to the ground. The flying hippogriff, half horse and half griffin, carried the Saracen knight (and sometime Paladin) **Roger** all the way around the globe, from France to France, with a rest stop in Japan. But the greatest of all horses was . . .

Rakhsh

The Persian warrior **Rostam** had muscles so large and weighty that most horses snapped in two underneath his frame. Finally, though, he managed to locate a colt the size of a camel that had the strength of an elephant. This was Rakhsh, the all-time champion horse. According to the *Shahnameh*, the book that spells it all out, Rakhsh was so smart and so perceptive that:

> He could discern the tiny emmet's foot
> Upon black cloth at night two leagues away.

Emmet just means *pismire*—an ant!—an ant's foot!—and two leagues is almost three miles. Rostam was once compelled to perform seven labors—more or less in the vein of Hercules's twelve—and the lucky guy didn't even have to *do* one of them, because Rakhsh beat him to it, killing a monstrous lion while Rostam slept.

We'll probably never know all the services a horse as wonderful as Rakhsh performed. Did Rakhsh write Rostam's term papers when he was studying at the Apprentice Academy? It's unclear, but perhaps there are some clues: a book report on Whinny the Pooh; a history paper on the Napoleonic general **Michel Neigh**; a home ec project that was just apples and sugar cubes . . .

Other Famous Horses

The Knight	The Horse
Alexander the Great	Bucephalus
Allard de Montauban	Bayard*
Amadis of Gaul	Bayard**
Bertrand	Clinevent
Bevis of Hampton	Arondel
Caligula	Incitatus, Consul of Rome
Cúchulainn	Dubh Sainglenn
Gawain	Gringolet
Guichard de Montauban	Bayard*
Guillaume d'Orange	Alion***
Guillaume d'Orange	Baucent***
Khosrow	Shabdiz
Louis of Vermandois	Ferrant
Manas	Manykär
Ogier the Dane	Broiefort
Renaud de Montauban	Bayard*
Richardet de Montauban	Bayard*
Roland	Veillantif****
Sacripant	Frontin
Sigurd	Grani
Witege	Schemming

*Bayard could magically elongate his back to permit all four Montaubons to ride him at once.

**Amadis rode Bayard, presumably in compact form, seven hundred years before the Montaubons.

***Guillaume's horses tended to die underneath him, so he had more than one.

****aka Brigliador.

After Bayard died, Renaud de Montaubon was so heartbroken he vowed never to ride a horse again. He gave up fighting altogether and spent old age building churches, until one day a group of stonemasons beat him to death for being better at it than they were.

The feline family

Even if your parents won't buy you a miraculous pony, you're not completely out of luck. There's a whole arkful of animals that aren't horses. In the Ayutthaya Kingdom of Thailand, legend says, warriors would go into battle with Siamese cats on their shoulders. The cats were trained to leap at opponents' faces, clawing and hissing, because there's no better way to get your opponent to drop their guard than the old cat-in-the-face trick. Cats are practically free! But even better than a cat is . . .

The lion: Yvain

Sir Yvain would have been just another knight, wandering around Arthurian Britain and hitting things when he got bored, but one day . . . he came across a dragon and a lion fighting. The dragon had the lion by the tail, and Yvain figured it was more chivalrous to assist the underdog, so he rode up, freed the lion by chopping off half its tail, and dispatched the dragon (perhaps using one of those weasel tricks I recommended earlier).

Yvain then turned to the lion, expecting to have to fight a second brute, but the grateful cat rolled on its back and soon the two were friends. The lion would go hunting and bring back deer and large game for Yvain to eat. Best of all, its cropped tail gave the lion a unique look, which was perfect for trademarks and licensing.

Together Sir Yvain and the lion fought, and defeated, a host of opponents up and down Britain, including:

1. The giant Harpin of the Mountain, who battered Yvain unconscious with his club before the lion came along and

mauled the giant into a coma. Then Yvain cut the giant's head off . . .

2. Three hostile knights simultaneously, which sounds really difficult—except Yvain only slew one of them before getting knocked unconscious, whereupon the lion ate the other two . . .

3. Two devils who ran a kind of sweatshop where hostage maidens did needlepoint in exchange for room and board, and not much board, while the devils raked in the big needlepoint bucks. The devils armed themselves with enormous maces fashioned from cherry dogwood trees wrapped in bands of copper and brass, but before they'd fight Yvain, they whined and moped and insisted that it was unfair for Yvain to fight them with the help of his lion. They went on and on about the unfairness of it all for so very long that finally Yvain grew sick of it and allowed the lion to be locked up in a high tower. Then the two devils beat Yvain mercilessly with their dogwood trees, until finally the lion managed to claw its way out of the tower, run to the castle yard, and kill the devils.

I'll grant that Yvain had to defeat a dragon, which is of course hard to do even with tricks, but you'll notice that he mainly coasted after that, focusing in each combat on staying alive long enough that his lion could come save him.

Kuskun Kara Mattyr

There's only one thing better than having a cool animal companion watching out for you, and that's being a cool animal companion yourself.

Kogutei, a warrior of the Altai Turks of Siberia, once found an orphaned young beaver shivering in the woods, and he took the rodent home with him and raised him as a son. The beaver proved his worth by fetching firewood—easier for beavers than most other

animals, that task—and furthermore learned to talk and ride a horse and fight with a sword and wear armor that had a flap for his tail. He took the name **Kuskun Kara Mattyr of the Raven Black Steed** and gained enough renown that he married a human woman, Karatty Kö, a princess of the khanate. I'm not sure how that worked, honestly, but they seemed to get along.

Nevertheless, Kuskun Kara Mattyr's in-laws treated him with the contempt one might employ when a rodent marries into the family. Finally, though, the in-laws' cattle were stolen, and only Kuskun Kara Mattyr proved able to win them back. He discovered that the cattle had been led away by the king of the birds—a creature known in Siberia by the name Khan Kerede, but, as birds do get around, famous in other lands by other appellations, such as the Simurgh, Garuda, Khyung, or the Ziz.

The warrior king Ortnit once chased a dragon off, thereby saving an elephant the dragon was menacing; the elephant in gratitude decided to follow Ortnit around, sharing his adventures. This sounds like an awesome setup, but unfortunately like five minutes later the dragon came back and ate both Ortnit and the elephant.

Whatever you choose to call him, the king of the birds, you must understand, will be difficult to catch, especially if you are a mammal more comfortable on land and water (such as a beaver) than in the air. Kuskun Kara Mattyr, instead of chasing down or attacking the bird king, went around helping out little birds—killing snakes before they could swallow birds' eggs, returning fallen unfledged chicks to their nests, etc. The bird king ended up so grateful for these acts of charity that he handed the cattle over to Kuskun Kara Mattyr with a tip of the hat and a wink of the eye.

If you want to lay the groundwork for a future deal with the king of the birds by various do-gooder ornithological deeds—I guess it can't hurt. It might be too late for you to be born as a beaver, though.

Human Companions

IF YOU CAN'T GET A GOOD ANIMAL COMPANION, YOU MIGHT AS WELL look for the next best thing, which is a human companion. Fortunately, humans are easy to find, as they turn up everywhere. And many of them are already sorted into confederations of knights that you can join, either as a junior auxiliary member while still at the Apprentice Academy or at a recruitment fair shortly before graduation.

Assembling the team

Joining an existing body of knights is one thing, but if you don't find one you like, or if everyone rejects you, you can always make your own.

A Maxim of the Fianna: To a chief do not abuse his people, for that is no work for a man of gentle blood.

This is not always easy, at least if you want to get really good knights on your side. **Hrolf Kraki**, king of Denmark, managed to assemble a legendary team of Viking warriors—some people call them the Kraklers, but never to their faces—by handing out gifts and rings more generously than other kings. But in order to pull this off, you need to be rich, of course, in gifts and rings, if in nothing else. If he were not already king of Denmark, Hrolf Kraki would have had a harder time being able to afford talent.

There is, however, a cheaper way to recruit, which we might call the Robin Hood Method.

Here's how it works: **Robin Hood** and a stranger once quarreled over who would cross a narrow bridge first. They came to blows, and the stranger won the contest, knocking Robin Hood into the river.

Robin Hood just laughed and invited the stranger to join his band of outlaws. And that's how Little John became a Merry Man.

Then another time Robin Hood went to rob a passing stranger. The stranger untied the bag he was carrying and reached in as though to pull out gold, but instead pulled out flour, for he was a miller, and threw the flour in Robin Hood's face. While Robin staggered around, blinded and choking, the stranger beat him into submission with his staff.

But Robin, once he recovered, just laughed and invited him to join his band of outlaws. And that's how Midge the Miller's Son became a Merry Man.

And yet another time, Robin Hood demanded a stranger carry him across a river on his back. The stranger carried him halfway and then tossed him into the river. Robin Hood went to attack the stranger, who blew a whistle and called a pack of war dogs that had been trained to catch arrows in their mouths and were thereby immune to Robin's archery.

Robin was delighted by this trick, and laughing, he invited the stranger to join his band of outlaws. And that's how Friar Tuck became a Merry Man.

Remember that becoming one of the Merry Men explicitly entailed leading a life of crime and sleeping in a tree. Presumably the fellowship you're recruiting for would have a more attractive clubhouse and not involve becoming wanted by the law, making recruitment even easier. All you need to do is endure humiliation and get your skull knocked around a bit.

> "Some lost legs and some lost arms,
>   And some did lose their blood,
>   But Robin Hood hee took up his noble bow,
>   And is gone to the merry green wood."
>
> –Child No. 139 (coll. 1860)

Joining the team

If the nonstop pain and humiliation of the Robin Hood Method sound unpleasant to you, you could always be the one who beats up Robin Hood, and then good-naturedly joins the team. There are plenty of teams to choose from: Jomsvikings, Nartsquad, the Forty-Seven Ronin. I guess some of these may have disbanded, although I haven't checked personally. Try one of these famous bands:

Merry Men

Founded: Late 12th century

Base of operations: Sherwood Forest

Primary House: Escallop

Notable leaders: Will Stutely, **Robin Hood**

Notable members:

Alan a Dale   Maid Marian
Arthur a Bland   Midge the Miller's Son
David of Doncaster   Wat the Tinker
Friar Tuck   Will Scarlet
Little John

The Forty Companions

Founded: 9th century

Base of operations: Kyrgyzstan

Primary House: A mix of Escallop and Biscione, maybe
some Martlet

Notable leader: **Manas**

Notable members:

Alaman Bet

Bok Murun

Er Koshoi

Er Töshtük

Jaipur

Jamgyrchi

Kös Kaman

Tas Baimat

Thirty-some-odd others

Knights of the Round Table

Founded: Late 5th century

Base of operations: Camelot

Primary House: Martlet

Notable leader: **King Arthur**

Notable members:

Sir Baldwin

Sir Bors

Sir Dinadan

Sir Galahad

Sir Gawain

Sir Kay

Sir Lamorak

Sir Lancelot

Merlin (sorcerer)

Sir Palamedes

King Pellinore

Sir Perceval

Sir Tom Thumb

Sir Yvain

Bogatyrs

Founded: 10th century

Base of operations: Kiev

Primary House: A mix of Martlet and Biscione

Notable leader: Vladimir

Notable members:

Alyosha Popovich	**Ilya Muromets**
Anna Ivanovna (sorcerer)	Solovei Budrinovich
	Svyatogor
Dobrynya Nikitich	Volga Vseslavich

Paladins

Founded: 8th century

Base of operations: Paris

Primary House: Martlet

Notable leader: Charlemagne

Notable members:

Astolf	**Renaud de Montauban**
Bradamante	**Roger**
Ganelon	**Roland**
Maugris (sorcerer)	**Thierry**
Ogier the Dane	Turpin
Oliver	

Kraklers

Founded: 6th century

Base of operations: Denmark

Primary House: Biscione

Notable leaders: **Hrolf Kraki**

Notable members:

Beygad
Bödvar Bjarki
Haklang
Haki the Valiant
Hardrefil
Hjalti

Hromund the Hard
Hrolf the Swift-Handed
Hvitserk the Bold
Storolf
Svipdag
Vott the Arrogant

Fianna

Founded: 3rd century

Base of operations: Ireland and Scotland

Primary House: Martlet

Notable leaders: Goll mac Morna, **Finn Mac Cool**

Notable members:

Conán mac Lia
Conán mac Morna
Diarmuid O'Duibhne

Geena mac Luga
Keelta mac Ronan
Oisin
Oscar

Okay, I did read that the Fianna disbanded. I read it on page 7 of this very book.

Buddies

Sometimes you don't need forty companions like **Manas**; sometimes you just need someone to watch your back when you travel, and to take turns carrying the food.

This could be a romantic couple, like the Paladins **Bradamante** and **Roger**, or a pair of buddies, like the Vikings **Hjalmar** and **Arrow-Odd**, or blood brothers, like (Paladins again) **Roland** and **Oliver**, or regular brothers, like **Garin le Loherain** and **Begon de Belin**, knights who lived two generations before the Paladins were formed.

But the original pairing was long ago in the earliest days of the Apprentice Academy, when **Gilgamesh** and **Enkidu** adventured together. Gilgamesh was a king, and Enkidu was a feral fellow who had grown up in the woods, and together they fought monsters and stirred up trouble across ancient Mesopotamia. It's really hard to defeat two knights if one of them is skilled in all the civilized arts of fencing and the other one is bitey, like a raccoon.

Seven thousand years after Gilgamesh and Enkidu, their team-up routine was copied by twin brothers named **Valentine** and **Orson**. They were Charlemagne's cousins, although they didn't learn that fact until much later, as their princess mother carelessly misplaced them both as infants. Valentine ended up as the ward of King Pepin of France—that's Charlemagne's father and Valentine's own uncle—and dutifully enrolled in the Apprentice Academy, House Martlet, while Orson (on the other hand) was adopted by a family of bears.

A baby taken in by bears is not so very unprecedented, at least among knights. Baby **Sayf Ben Dhi Yazan** was suckled by an antelope, baby **Basat** by a lioness, and baby Romulus by a wolf. But Sayf Ben Dhi Yazan, Basat, and Romulus only hung out with their animal mothers long enough for an enterprising human to pick them

up and raise them, while Orson stayed among bears until he was grown, eating honey and berries and mauling passersby.

Valentine's senior project at A.A. was to go and kill that horrible wild man who'd been terrorizing the countryside like some kind of human-shaped bear. But when Valentine and Orson fought, some flicker of kinship—the twins did look exactly alike, except that only one of them had ever had a bath—stopped the combat. Valentine and Orson became friends. A few night classes at A.A. for Orson—House Escallop, naturally—and soon the wild man was able to swing a sword and wear armor, where once he had fought naked and armed only with his own fingernail claws.

Orson's burgeoning skill served the duo well when Valentine entered into single combat with a giant dressed all in green armor. Any wound the giant received would heal immediately, and it turned out he could only be permanently injured by a knight who had never been nursed on a woman's milk—a description that hardly applied to Valentine, nor to any of the last sixteen knights the giant had slain, nor, in fact, to almost any knight in France.

Except Orson, who had tasted only bear milk—and, maybe later on, after he grew up, with cookies, cow milk. The giant battered Valentine until he staggered away from the combat, and Orson quickly took up his brother's arms. Now that they had both bathed, the two knights looked alike, so the giant in green assumed the knight that now faced him was Valentine, returned for more.

It was not, and that was the end of the giant in green.

So this is my advice: If by chance you have had the good fortune to have been raised by bears or other animals deep in the woods, perhaps you would be well served by teaming up with a civilized knight, perhaps of House Martlet, for maximum contrast. And if you are, which is more likely, a civilized knight, perhaps you could find a man-eating, half-crazed human beast to team up with. It's almost as good as having an animal companion!

Quests

WHAT DO KNIGHTS DO WHEN THEY'RE NOT STABBING EACH OTHER? MOST of the time, they're going on quests.

This activity often seems absurd. **King Pellinore**, until he died of old age, spent all his free time questing after the so-called Questing Beast, a creature whose primary characteristic was that it could never be found. Maybe don't take that quest.

Before you quest

The first thing to do, before you even pack for a quest, is to arrange for someone to watch over you as you go. Unless your quest takes place in your backyard, such watching-over may require a magical alarm of sorts. Take three quick examples:

The Nyanga hero **Mwindo**, before he left on a quest to plunder the Underworld, gave his aunt a piece of magic rope, telling her that as long as the rope kept writhing, she would know he was alive. If the rope stopped writhing, that meant he was dead.

You know what? After Pellinore's death. **Sir Palamedes** actually managed to find, and slay, the Questing Beast. You never know what's going to happen!

The Nart hero **Warzameg**, before he left on a quest to steal cattle from the land of Chinta, gave his wife a magic hole punch and told her to punch a hole in her palm occasionally. If milk came out of the wound, she would know he was alive. If blood came, that meant he was dead.

The Finnish hero **Lemminkäinen**, before he left on a quest to win the hand of the princess of Pohjola, gave his mother a magic hairbrush, telling her that as long as the brush did nothing weird, she would know he was alive. If the hairbrush began to bleed, that meant he was dead.

As it turned out, only Lemminkäinen ever needed rescuing—he was killed by a snake and subsequently dismembered; his mother used a magical rake to drag all his pieces up from the Underworld and subsequently stitched him back together—but such an alarm is good insurance for everyone.

"He questions all men of the Beast.
None answer. Is the quest in vain?"

—Crowley, *Good Sir Palamedes* (1912)

Quests: Been there, done that

The problem with quests is that so many of them have already been completed. **Sir Galahad**, Sir Bors, and **Sir Perceval** already found the Holy Grail. **Culhwch** already found the comb and scissors of the poisonous boar (!) Twrch Trwyth (watch out!). **Jason** and the Argonauts already found the Golden Fleece. You can't just go look for the Golden Fleece again.

Actually, I guess you can, because Jason found it three millennia ago, and it's probably been lost since then. But you know what I mean.

Fortunately, there's one place that quester after quester has gone to, and it's always there for more. Why not go on a quest that will take you to the Underworld? **Odysseus** did it to consult with the dead seer Tiresias. **Sir Orfeo** did it, to reclaim his dead wife Heurodis. **Mwindo** did it, one short page ago. Everyone's doing it. The technical term here is *harrowing*. Everyone's harrowing the Underworld.

Unfortunately, as the Sibyl told **Aeneas**,

"The gates of hell are open night and day;
Smooth the descent, and easy is the way:
But to return, and view the cheerful skies,
In this the task and mighty labor lies."

How to *get out* of the Underworld once your quest is over—that's the kind of top-quality information you can only get from a book like this.

Er Töshtük

After a giant-jawed monster called Jelmogus stole **Er Töshtük**'s soul and carried it with her to the Underworld, the soulless Er Töshtük tracked her there on his magical talking steed, Chal Kuiruk. He quested around in the Underworld but found that, although Chal Kuiruk was magical enough to gallop back to its home in Kyrgyzstan above, it was unable to bear Er Töshtük with it. Er Töshtük was trapped in the Land of the Dead.

Refusing to despair, Er Töshtük wandered the Underworld until he found a dragon menacing an eagle's aerie. Er Töshtük slew the dragon (probably by means of a cunning trick) and in return the eagle offered to fly Er Töshtük out of the Underworld. The only catch was, it was going to be a long flight, and the eagle needed food to keep its strength up. Er Töshtük's job was to feed it as it flew.

Er Töshtük packed up a bunch of food for the journey. But food is heavy, and the more food he brought the harder the eagle was going to need to labor to keep aloft, and the hungrier it would get. Er Töshtük had to do a lot of math to plan out the most efficient amount of food to bring. But eventually they started on their way.

And so they flew, Er Töshtük huddled on the eagle's back, popping morsels into its beak as they went. But the food dwindled and still the eagle had not managed to leave the deeps of the Underworld. And then, just like that, the last morsel was gone.

"We're almost there. But I hunger," said the eagle.

"Are you absolutely sure," Er Töshtük asked, "that you need more food?"

"In a moment I'm going to pass out and then we'll crash, and both die," said the eagle. So Er Töshtük removed his left eye and fed it to the eagle.

A Maxim of' the Fianna: Dispense thy meat freely.

A little while later he cut a chunk out of his left shoulder, and the eagle ate that, too. But then they were home.

How to get out of the Underworld: Befriend an eagle and bring along lots of dumplings with helium in the middle instead of meat so you can carry lots and lots of them without weighing yourself down. (Actually, I guess if you carry enough helium dumplings, you don't even need to befriend an eagle.)

King Arthur

Early in his career, **King Arthur** and a large cadre of knights sailed in Arthur's magic ship *Fair Shape* west across the seas until they reached the Underworld. Their quest had two objectives—the rescue of a prisoner named Gweir and the plundering of a remarkable cauldron, probably the cauldron of Diwrnach, and . . .

Look, it's hard to tell exactly what happened. Surviving records are fragmentary and confusing. They got the cauldron, maybe they got Gweir—whose name looks a lot like a shortening of *Guinevere*, doesn't it?—there was a lot of deadly fighting, and of all the knights who went on the quest, only seven returned from the Underworld. The whole experience was so traumatic that Arthur never mentioned it again. It was probably a huge mistake.

But Arthur had that magic ship, and even with almost all his knights dead in the Underworld, he was able to hop into *Fair Shape* with the survivors and make it back to Camelot.

When **Culhwch** (years later) asked Arthur for a favor, Arthur said he would gladly give Culhwch anything he owned with some exceptions: and he listed those exceptions, things such as his sword, Excalibur, and his favorite dog, and his shield decorated with an image of Our Lady, and—*Fair Shape*, his magic ship. Always keep the magic ship.

How to get out of the Underworld: Have a magic ship. (Maybe procure one from King Arthur by asking him for a favor and then cutting him off with "Could I have your magic ship?" before he manages to get to the magic ship exception.)

Pirithous and Theseus

Pirithous and **Theseus** decided to travel to the Land of the Dead and kidnap its queen, Persephone. Pirithous had the idea that he'd like to marry a goddess, and it seemed easier to get to the Underworld than to climb to Olympus. Theseus just went along because he and Pirithous liked to adventure together. They were (as they say) friends to the end.

The two heroes made the long trek to the Underworld. The way was easy and the descent was smooth, just as the Sibyl claimed, but even though it was easy and smooth, it was still a long way—it turns out the Underworld is really big—and eventually Pirithous and Theseus sat on a rock to rest. They found themselves unable to rise. They were stuck fast to the rock!

Sometime later, **Hercules**, who had come to the Underworld to fetch the three-headed dog Cerberus, found Pirithous and Theseus sitting on a rock.

"What are you doing here?" Hercules asked. "You missed the Quest for the Golden Fleece!"

"Do you think you could pull us off the rock?" was all they'd say.

So Hercules grabbed Theseus and gave a mighty heave. Part of Theseus's buttocks remained stuck to the rocks, but the rest of him tore free.

Next Hercules turned his attention to Pirithous, but no matter how hard he pulled, Pirithous, who was, after all, the guiltier party, remained stuck to the rock.

Finally, Hercules and Theseus gave up and decided to leave.

"Hey," said Pirithous, "I thought we were friends to the end."

"I've left my end on the rock with you," Theseus explained, gesturing to the chunks of his buttocks.

"You can't leave me behind," Pirithous said.

"No, no," said Theseus. "I have merely left you my behind."

And they quibbled in an amusing fashion like this until finally Theseus tired of the game and departed. Pirithous stayed behind on a rock in the Underworld. Apparently forever.

How to get out of the Underworld: Betray your friends. (Come to think of it, that is also a good way to get *into* the Underworld. A twofer!)

The Underworld sounds awful, and what if I want to go on a different quest?

One of the greatest quests still available to an enterprising young knight involves coming to my house and doing my laundry. I know it sounds like a stupid quest, but the laundry is . . . it's legendary laundry, okay? Also, you could mow my legendary lawn. Please address serious inquiries only in care of this publisher.

Maybe you could also write the next book in this series and put my name on it? We can talk.

The Code

AN OLD POEM DESCRIBES **SIR ORFEO** AS

"A stalwart man and hardy bo,
Large and courteous he was also."

Large here means "generous" (not sure what *bo* means, frankly). There's more to being a knight than just being stalwart and hardy. In other words, a knight is more than just a soldier. Partially this is because knights kill dragons and own magical swords, but partially this is because knights live by certain rules. *Generosity* and *courtesy* may slay no dragons, but they may well be part of *the code*.

Codes can be very simple. The Viking raiders who followed **Hjalmar** lived their lives bound by three rules only:

1. Don't eat raw meat, even with the juice squeezed out.

2. Don't steal from ladies.

3. Don't steal from peasants *unless you really need something bad.*

That's not the hardest set of rules, frankly. I very rarely eat raw meat anyway, just from personal preference.

Other knights, though, decided to live their lives by a baroque system of regulations known as . . .

Chivalry

A chivalrous knight must be brave on the battlefield, must never back down from a fight, must always uphold the side of the weak, must never take unfair advantage, blah blah blah. There are so many rules!

And the rules are all *local*, which means that every culture has its own version of them. In Japan, samurai live by the code of *Bushido*, which is similar to chivalry but subtly different in ways I don't even really understand. You can knock yourself out learning all that chivalry entails and then you're visiting Japan and you have to learn Bushido? This is all too hard!

I would never tell you that you shouldn't be chivalrous, or courteous, or kind to puppies or whatever. But I am obliged to point out that chivalry has a weakness, which is that *it is incredibly easy to take advantage of*.

A knight named **Sir Gasozein de Dragoz** once kidnapped Queen Guinevere (as, I repeat, was the custom), and **Sir Gawain** engaged him in mounted combat as part of a rescue mission. The two knights fought until Gasozein's horse wearied and fell over. Gasozein was so angry at his horse that he decapitated it. Gawain instantly killed his own horse, too, explaining (to a shocked Guinevere who was standing nearby) that he only did it to ensure that he would not have an unfair advantage over Gasozein.

Did Gasozein immediately go: "Oops," and drop his sword down a well, forcing the chivalrous Gawain also to drop his sword down a well—whereupon he could say that Gawain would have to try to rescue the kidnapped queen at a later date, because now no one had swords?

No, but he sure could have!

Likewise, if you were to go tomorrow to your Apprentice Academy instructor and point out that they have the answer key and you do not and how chivalrous is that? . . . well, you never know until you try.

Karna, son of the sun god, was born wearing the Kavach, a suit of magical armor that was attached to his skin and which protected him from all harm. Since Karna was also a great archer and a deadly swordsman — well, who would want to fight a great archer and deadly swordsman even if he were not immune to all harm?

But India at the time was divided by war, and Karna was fated to fight **Arjuna** — also a great archer and also the son of a god. Arjuna would have no chance as long as Karna was wearing his Kavach. So you'd think this whole thing was settled.

But of course, Karna was chivalrous. One day he was heading to the river to take a bath — wearing his Kavach, naturally, because it was a part of him — when a mendicant friar asked Karna for some alms.

"I'm so sorry," said Karna. "But I have nothing to give you. I'm on my way to the bath, you see."

The friar looked sheepish. "Well," he said, "you do have that armor . . ."

"I'm not sure," said Karna, "that I'll be able to —"

"Here's a knife," said the friar.

So, using the knife, Karna peeled from his flesh the invincible armor, which he handed over to the friar — who *ho ho!* was actually Arjuna's divine father in disguise! *ha ha!* — and off he went to the river to bathe his wounds.

Later, Karna and Arjuna fought, and it was a tough fight, but Karna had no invincible armor to prevent Arjuna from cutting off his head with a magic arrow, so that's exactly what happened.

Karna earned immortal fame and glory for his generosity, but I can't help but point out that I would have handled things a little differently.

"I dried my tears & armd my fears,
With ten thousand shields and spears."

—Blake, *Songs of Experience* (1794)

Chivalry is all well and good, but it can be seen as more of a House Martlet thing. It doesn't *have* to be for House Martlet—you'll notice how chivalrous the maxims of the Fianna are, and those moss-kissers are almost all Escallop—but chivalry is at heart a custom, and some houses have their own customs. House Biscione, for example, has . . .

Boasting

When **Beowulf** showed up at the great hall of Heorot, the first thing he did was tell everyone how great he was at everything. One man, Unferth, stood up to question some of his claims—Beowulf asserted he swam the seas for seven days and nights in full armor, a sword in one hand with which he slew sea monsters, and maybe that's a little hard to swallow—but Beowulf cited his sources and backed up all his claims and maybe flexed his muscles a little. Are you really going to call Beowulf a liar? He fought sea monsters for seven days straight, so calling him a liar sounds dangerous!

A Maxim of the Fianna: Be not talkative nor rashly censorious.

Beowulf is House Biscione, so boasting is in his blood. It's the first thing he does when he walks in the door, and he's good enough at it that Unferth scampers away with his tail between his legs.

You can try this, too, and maybe you have to fight sea monsters ahead of time, and maybe you don't.

» Cet mac Mágach

The first thing to do to gain skill at boasting is to lay some groundwork. Here is one of the all-time classic boast battles, as waged at a feast served by Mac Da Thó, king of Leinster.

Many a tough and bravo had been invited to the feast, and when the main course was served, each of them vied for the right to carve the pork. **Cet mac Mágach** stood before the plate with carving knife in hand, while warrior after warrior stood up to take

113

the knife from him, but every time Cet would shoot the newcomer down, simply by talking.

Óengus stood up, and Cet mentioned the time he had cut off Óengus's father's hand. Óengus sat down. Éogan stood up, and Cet mentioned the time he had stolen all of Éogan's cattle and put out one of Éogan's eyes. Éogan sat down. And so it went, with Cet outbragging them all, until **Conall Cernach** walked through the door.

"Okay, fine," Cet said. "You're a better fighter than I am, I'll admit it. But if my brother Anlúan were in the hall, you'd see who was so tough. Too bad he's not here."

Conall Cernach had prepared for just such a moment. "Ah," he said, "Anlúan is closer than you think." He opened up his pouch and *pulled out Anlúan's head.*

That's good boasting! A visual aid is always nice.

"I'm the double-jawed hyena from the East.
I'm the blazing, bloody blizzard of the States."

—Lomax, *Cowboy Songs* (coll. 1910)

» Kara Tygan Khan

If boasting were just a way for Conall Cernach to step on Cet mac Mágach, it would be no more important than bowling scores or fire safety. Boasting actually serves a purpose, though. Boasting *gives knights something to do.*

At his wedding, the Kachin Turkish warrior **Kara Tygan Khan** got so excited he vowed to restore two dead brothers, Altyn and Kümüs Ergäk, to life. This impressed everyone, of course, as a good brag should.

But the next morning, Kara Tygan Khan woke up with a problem.

"How are you going to do it?" his new wife asked.

"How are you going to do it?" his new brother-in-law asked.

"Wait, what did I promise to do?" said Kara Tygan Khan, rubbing his temples.

And indeed, instead of spending a pleasant day unwrapping wedding presents, Kara Tygan Khan found himself heading out in search of a way to resurrect two dead guys.

He finally found it, far away in the Altai Mountains, where a restorative herb grows at the top of a great pine tree guarded by monstrous ravens. So that was good luck for the Ergäk brothers!

But here you see the basic life cycle of an adventure. A knight in their cups or at a moment of great excitement says they're going to do something crazy and impossible . . . and then they're stuck! Step two is the quest, and then there's a moment's respite before they're making another crazy boast. Not long after Kara Tygan Khan had returned from the Altai Mountains, he started talking big in front of the sorcerer Suksagal Khan, whereupon the sorcerer ended up stealing Kara Tygan Khan's eyes, and . . .

Look, it just never ends. That's the life you've signed up for.

» Jomsvikings

The Jomsvikings were a group of mercenaries who lived on the coast of Pomerania, which gave them the whole Baltic Sea as their stomping ground. The Jomsvikings had their own charter of rules that they had to follow—avenge your fellows' deaths, don't squabble with other Jomsvikings, etc.—although Jomsvikings were not always the best at following rules, even their own. One rule held that to join the Jomsvikings one must be between the ages of eighteen and fifty, but when a twelve-year-old orphan named **Vagn Akason** showed up at their door, the Jomsvikings said he could join if he defeated in single combat their champion, **Sigvaldi Strut-Haraldsson**. Much to everyone's surprise, especially Sigvaldi's, Vagn won the contest, and soon he was a

Jomsviking, in contravention of their laws. But because they had broken their own charter, the Jomsvikings fell into internal dispute and a lengthy series of wars.

So this charter was important, but more important to the operation of the Jomsvikings was their custom of boasting, and this custom led to their downfall.

It happened, as it often does, at a banquet. The Jomsviking stronghold of Jomsborg had recently been recognized as an independent state by the king of Denmark—Jomsvikings had kidnapped the king and held him hostage until he recognized their sovereignty, because that's the way Jomsvikings operated—and everyone was in the mood to celebrate.

After several hours of crapulence, Sigvaldi Strut-Haraldsson stood up and spontaneously boasted that before three years had passed, he would invade Norway and either slay or exile its ruler, Jarl Hakon. Not coincidentally, Jarl Hakon was the king of Denmark's enemy.

His brother **Thorkill the High** then stood up and declared that he, too, would invade Norway, and that he would never flee from battle as long as his brother was still fighting.

Then **Bui Digre** stood up and declared that he would invade Norway as well, and would never flee from battle as long as both Sigvaldi and Thorkill were still fighting.

Then Bui's son, **Sigurd Fairhair**, also arose and declared his intent to invade Norway, never fleeing as long as Sigvaldi, Thorkill, Bui, and one third of the Jomsvikings remained in combat.

Then Vagn Akason, a little older now, vowed to sail with them to Norway, murder the Norwegian nobleman Thorkill Leira, and marry Leira's beautiful daughter Ingaborg.

Soon everyone was vowing all sorts of things, generally involving Norway. It was a wonderful party!

Of course, the next day the Jomsvikings woke up realizing they had declared war on an entire country.

Sigvaldi couldn't back out, as he had made the vow. And Thorkill the High couldn't back out as long as Sigvaldi didn't back out. And Bui Digre couldn't back out as long as Sigvaldi and Thorkill the High didn't back out. And Sigurd Fairhair couldn't back out as long as Sigvaldi and Thorkill the High and Bui Digre and one third of the Jomsvikings weren't backing out. And one third of the Jomsvikings weren't about to back out! Everyone was going.

But there are reasons people don't plan invasions based on tipsy boasting. The invasion was a disaster, as the Jomsvikings faced both other Vikings and black magic. Sigvaldi Strut-Haraldsson did end up turning tail and fleeing, despite his vows, and Thorkill the High got to flee because Sigvaldi fled. Bui Digre jumped into the sea when his ship was boarded and turned into an underwater dragon somehow. And everyone else ended up in the next chapter, "Dying Well."

Bravery

The common wellspring of chivalry, Bushido, or just about any knightly code, is the concept of bravery. Knights love to be brave!

The Yankton Sioux of South Dakota still speak of the Battalion of Death, a group of warriors who had vowed never to retreat, nor swerve from their course when on the way to battle. This battalion was crossing an iced-over Missouri River when it came upon a hole in the ice, right in front of it. The warriors could have gone around the hole, of course, but they had vowed not to swerve from their course, and marched directly forward, toward the hole. The leader of the Battalion of Death fell into the icy river and was swept away, and the first rank would have followed him had not the Yankton warriors from other battalions tackled them.

"Be bolde, Be bolde, and everywhere, Be bolde."

—Spenser, *Faerie Queene* (1590)

According to the Roman historian Aelian, the warriors of Gaul considered it cowardice to retreat even from a burning building, or the encroaching tide.

Knights (we have already seen) are loath to retreat. Generally, this is simply a matter of honor, or chivalry, or Bushido—in other words an arbitrary standard, like selecting the right fork at a meal.

The aged knight **Sir Baldwin**, though, laid out (in response to questions from **King Arthur**) what appear to be rational reasons for being brave.

The case for bravery: Sir Baldwin

Baldwin explained to the king that in the days of Arthur's grandfather, King Constantine, Sir Baldwin himself had been in a besieged castle. While Baldwin and other knights went out on sallies against the besiegers, or walked the parapets to knock down siege ladders, one of his fellow knights decided to cower in an empty barrel. Much safer in a barrel!

It transpired, though, that a catapult hurled a stone into the castle, and that stone struck the top off the barrel. It also struck the top off the cowering knight: While his body remained among the shattered barrel staves, his head was found a hundred yards away, squished flat under the missile.

"On that day I learned," Sir Baldwin explained, "that death can come for you anywhere, so you may as well face it bravely."

The case against bravery: Sir Baldwin reexamined

Look, I'm not trying to speak ill of a Knight of the Table Round, but the truth is Sir Baldwin is just bad at math.

If you flip a coin, it might come down heads, and it might come down tails, and it might get snapped up in midair by a crow who carries it to his nest on the top of a forbidden tower made of ice. Any of these things might happen.

But if we're going to flip a coin, and instead of calling heads or

118

tails you call snapped up in midair by a crow who carries it to his nest on the top of a forbidden tower made of ice, you're probably going to lose (although, once every hundred thousand flips, you'll look *really impressive*).

Baldwin is correct that death can come to you as you hide in a barrel, and it can come to you as you charge into battle against a superior foe . . . but what you should be worrying about is *which is more likely*.

Problem solving in practice: Hrolf Kraki

Hrolf Kraki and his team of Kraklers visited the castle of the treacherous Swedish king Adils, but Adils, being Adils, set his own castle on fire in an attempt to kill the Kraklers.

Here you see the dilemma Hrolf and his Kraklers were in. If they run away from something as small as a fire, they will be revealed as cowards. If they stay where they are, they burn to cinders.

But Hrolf Kraki didn't become a legendary Viking leader for nothing. He jumped over the flames, while explaining, in case anyone was about to point a finger, "He flees not the fire who leaps over it!"

His companions jumped over the fire, too, and ran toward King Adils—who himself fled, through the use of a magic tree, which hardly seems sporting.

But if you ever find yourself in trouble and have to run away, try the Hrolf Kraki method and *explain why you're not running away as you run away*.

> "The bullets fly at random where they list,
> And should I go and kill a thousand men
> I were as soon rewarded with a shot,
> As sooner far than he that never fights."
>
> —Marlowe, *Tamburlaine the Great* (1587)

Dying Well

WAIT. DON'T GET AHEAD OF YOURSELF. A TRUE KNIGHT (THEY TELL ME) never gives up.

When **Cúchulainn** and **Ferdiad** waged their famous duel at the ford, Ferdiad's sword hacked hunks of flesh the size of babies' heads (sources tell us) from Cúchulainn's body. Cúchulainn suffered wounds so large that a bird could have flown right through one of them, the way (sources tell us) a bird flies through the window in a wall. And of course, still, Cúchulainn did not give up.

At the 1388 Battle of Chevy Chase, **Richard Witherington** . . . well, the old ballad puts it succinctly:

"For Witherington needs must I wayle,
    As one in doleful dumpes
For when his legges were smitten off,
    He fought upon his stumpes."

But sometimes, even when you don't give up, life gives up for you. Sometimes you're just going to die. *C'est la guerre*, they say, which more or less means: "What did you expect when you started chopping people up with a sword?" No knight lives forever —

Well, **Ogier the Dane** does, sleeping eternally in the basement

120

of the castle of Kronenburg, an iron crown on his head keeping him from aging—but most knights die eventually. Don't blame me.

So you're going to die

In which case, why not die well? It will vex your enemies, at the very least. The Bourbons put Napoleon's daring general **Michel Ney** in front of a firing squad, and Ney insisted on giving the order to fire himself. He also lectured the squad where to aim. Ney died when he called "fire," but the Bourbons were *furious*!

Some thousand years earlier, after the treasonous Acelin failed to usurp the French throne, **Guillaume d'Orange** refused to let the traitor be executed with a sword, saying it would be a scandal to give such a man an honorable death. Instead, Guillaume beat him to death with a stick, as one might beat a donkey, or a rug.

A Maxim of the Fianna: Utter not swaggering speech, nor say thou wilt not yield what is right; it is a shameful thing to speak too stiffly unless that it be feasible to carry out thy words.

I guess on the one hand it doesn't matter whether you die like Ney or like Acelin. On the other hand, if you have to go, you might as well go in a way that irritates someone.

Starkad, a warrior so tough that he was born with eight arms, and only lost six of them when *Thor himself* pulled them off in a fight, kept growing older and weaker, and he realized that despite the life of danger and recklessness he had led, he was in real peril of dying peacefully in bed. How was he going to irritate someone that way?

So Starkad sought out a youth named Hather. "Kid," said Starkad. And he explained that he was the one who had killed the lad's father, and furthermore stolen the man's gold. But Starkad was offering to return the gold—it's in this pouch here—and give Hather an opportunity to avenge his dad. All Hather had to do was strike off

Starkad's head. Starkad would even lend him a sword to do it with. And—here was the kicker—if after swinging the sword Hather was able to jump between Starkad's body and his tumbling head, then his skin would thereafter be immune to all wounds. "How about it, kid?"

So Hather swung the sword and chopped off Starkad's head, but instead of trying to jump forward, between the head and the body, he jumped backward, and good thing, too, because Starkad's enormous bulk, still hulking and heavy despite his advanced age, pitched forward in death, and would have crushed the lad beneath it had he not leaped clear.

Nice try, though, Starkad. It was a nice try.

Roland

There is, of course, a fine line between dying well and being a dunce.

Charlemagne was leading the French army out of Spain, its rear guard captained by **Roland**, greatest of Charlemagne's Paladins, and beside him his blood brother **Oliver**. An enormous force from Saragossa ambushed the rear guard at Roncevaux Pass, and the outnumbered Frenchmen soon found themselves in a pickle.

"Fortunately," said Oliver, "Charlemagne and the rest of the French army is nearby. Roland, do you wind your Oliphant"—for this was the name of the horn Roland had plundered from the corpse of the warrior **Aumon**—"and they'll come to our aid."

But Roland just scoffed, because he believed in the code. It must have been a weird code, because once, when Orlando was spurned by a visiting damsel from the East, he went completely nuts and rampaged across Europe and Africa for three months, straight-up murdering anyone he met. You'd think murdering random people constantly for three months would be against some kind of code—but Roland was House Biscione, and I guess it made sense at the time. Nevertheless, there would be no call for reinforcements.

And now, here in Roncevaux Pass, Roland and Oliver fought

side by side. All around them the rest of the rear guard fell in heaps. Roland and Oliver were dreadfully outnumbered.

"Perhaps the Oliphant?" Oliver suggested. But Roland insisted he was no coward.

Finally, though, finally it became clear that every last French knight was going to die—and perhaps Oliver's hectoring had grown intolerable. Finally, Roland agreed to wind his Oliphant and summon the main French army . . . but of course the fighting had been going on for hours, and by now Charlemagne was out of earshot. Roland blew and blew again, but no answering sound came. Nobody had heard.

You must know that Roland hated to fail in any deed, even if the deed he was failing in was blowing a horn. So he took one last deep breath and managed to sound the horn louder and longer than ever a horn had been sounded. The strain was so great that Roland popped the blood vessels in his temples. Blood shot out of his head; it shot out of his nose and mouth. He staggered around, and while he was busy staggering, Saragossan soldiers surrounded Oliver and stabbed him in the back.

Oliver turned around, got his revenge on the fellow who stabbed him and then died. Roland staggered around some more, failed to break his sword, and died from blood loss. Only then did Charlemagne's army show up.

They had to send word to **Renaud de Montauban** back in France and tell him he was now the greatest of King Charlemagne's Paladins.

Guys, guys. Maybe just blow the horn, okay? Especially if you're going to end up doing it anyway. Blowing a horn is like putting milk in the fridge—you're better off doing it *right away*.

The Nibelungs

The Burgundian heroes known as the Nibelungs once got lured into a trap by **Attila the Hun** and were captured. Many a Nibelung was

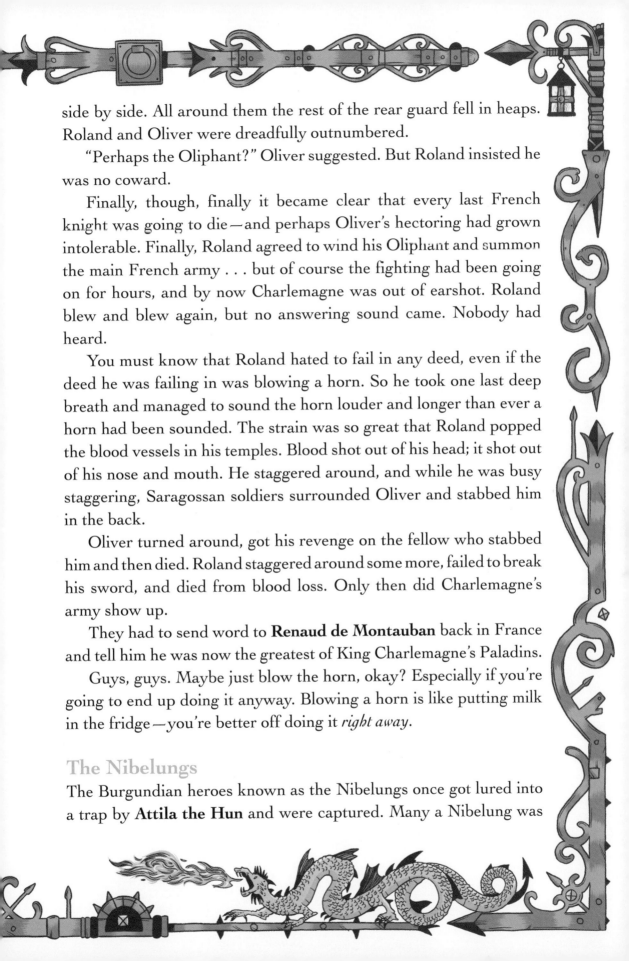

killed by Huns when the trap was sprung, but King **Gunther** and the dour warrior **Hagen** were taken captive. Attila desired the magnificent treasure hoard known as the Rheingold, which the Nibelungs had left behind in Burgundy, and offered to spare the life of whoever told him its location.

"I'll tell you," Gunther offered Attila, "on the condition that you bring me Hagen's heart on a platter."

Attila sought to deceive Gunther by killing a scullery boy and bringing his heart in, platter and all. But Gunther took one look at the heart and saw that it was quivering.

"Hagen's heart never trembled," Gunther said, which you may notice kind of destroys the whole purpose of hearts. But in this case, he was right, and Attila had to admit it. The Hun sent his men to the cell of the prisoner Hagen. They cut his heart out of his living breast, and Hagen just laughed at them the whole time.

Attila presented the heart to Gunther. And now it was Gunther's turn to laugh. He laughed and laughed, and Attila asked why.

"Because now you'll never get your hands on the Rheingold, sucker!" Gunther crowed. "Only two people in the entire world knew its secret location, Hagen and I—*and I'll never tell!*"

Gunther kept laughing as Attila had him tossed into a pit filled with poison snakes with his hands bound behind his back. He found an old harp down there in the pit—clearly Gunther was not the first person to feed these snakes—and although his hands were bound, he managed to play the harp with his toes, charming the snakes with his music. This could only go on for so long, and eventually a harp string broke, a snake bit Gunther, and serpentdom assembled ate him up.

A death like that is hard to beat. But it's been beaten . . .

The Jomsvikings

At the Battle of Hjorungavagr, the Jomsvikings (you may recall) were defeated by the forces of Jarl Hakon of Norway (who incidentally

sacrificed his son to Odin to gain the magical powers that secured the victory, so . . . not a fair fight). The few survivors found themselves bound together in a row, sitting on a log, while Hakon's man Thorkill Leira came with an ax, decapitating one after another. When the axman got to **Sigurd Fairhair**, Sigurd requested that he be permitted to keep his luxurious blond locks in perfect condition, even into death. "Let not blood sully my hair," and all that.

> "This is the way to live—that when thou diest
>
> No one believes that thou art really dead."
>
> —Le Gallienne, *Odes* (1903)

So Thorkill Leira sighed, "Fine," and ordered one of his men, Ragnvald, to hold Sigurd's beautiful hair away from his neck. Sigurd bowed his head. Ragnvald stood there, his hands full of blond hair, looking bored. Thorkill raised the ax.

And as the ax fell, Sigurd jerked his body back, pulling Ragnvald off balance. The ax missed Sigurd's neck but came down into his hair, also into Ragnvald's arms. Sigurd was left with a short haircut—a kind of a bob. Ragnvald was left with no hands.

This is pretty terrible, but of course Vikings, being Vikings, found this manner of sport hilarious. Jarl Hakon's other son, Erik, couldn't stop laughing, but he finally managed to gasp out that the entertainment was so delightful that the Jomsvikings could go free.

Thorkill Leira, for understandable reasons mentioned several pages ago, countered that the other Jomsvikings may receive his mercy, but **Vagn Akason** would receive only an ax blow. Thorkill charged toward Vagn . . . but Vagn and the man next to him dived in opposite directions so that the rope that bound the two together

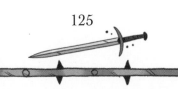

drew taut. Thorkill promptly tripped over the rope, dropping his ax, which bounced over toward Vagn. A lucky Vagn cut his bonds, picked up the ax, and went to get revenge on Thorkill—but Erik, son of the Jarl, came over still laughing and said that peace had already been called, and everyone should just cut it out.

And—holy crow, it worked! The Jomsvikings died so well that they didn't die at all! They just got to go home.

"Come squire and dwarf, the Sun grows towards his set,

And we have many more adventures yet."

—Beaumont, *Knight of the Burning Pestle* (1607)

Appendix A: Ezechiacon

Twenty-eight-hundred years ago, one King Hezekiah compiled a list of all the magic items he could think of. The whole reason for the list was that Hezekiah believed magic items were too dangerous to exist—this was just his checklist of things he wanted to track down and destroy. Nevertheless, ever since then a catalog of magical items has been called an Ezechiacon. This brief sampler lists some weapons, armor, and miscellaneous trappings that knights have used or been subjected to.

Argalia's Lance
COMES FROM: Cathay
OWNED BY: Astolf

This lance will unhorse any knight it strikes. Argalia used it in a tournament (which sounds like cheating) with the understanding that in any joust, the loser would be the winner's captive. First Argalia defeated the English knight Astolf, and so Astolf agreed to serve Argalia, as the rules stated. Next Argalia defeated Ferragut, a knight who cared nothing for tournament rules. He was just angry to have been defeated, and attacked Argalia with a sword. While the two were fighting, Astolf snuck over, picked up the lance, and used it to become Europe's number one jouster (which also sounds like cheating—but who am I to judge?). (*Orlando Innamorato*.)

Armor of Zarosht

COMES FROM: Persia
OWNED BY: Esfandiyar

Esfandiyar's enchanted armor, the gift of a holy man, protects the wearer from all harm except being shot in both eyes simultaneously with a double-headed arrow. Since it's almost impossible to shoot someone in both eyes simultaneously with a double-headed arrow, Esfandiyar felt pretty safe, even when fighting against Rostam, one of the deadliest knights in history. Unfortunately for Esfandiyar, Rostam turned out to be really good at shooting people in both eyes simultaneously with a double-headed arrow. (*Shahmaneh.*)

Boomerang of the Rainmaker

COMES FROM: Australia
OWNED BY: Djunban

This deadly boomerang slays whomever it hits. You may think that this is a particularly dangerous power to have *in a boomerang* of all things, but before Djunban could accidentally hit himself with it, he accidentally hit his sister, who didn't die until after she had buried the accursed thing. (Wiranggu-Kokatato myth.)

Bow of the King of the Wind

COMES FROM: Cambodia
OWNED BY: Kaundinya

When Kaundinya warred with Willow Leaf, princess of the Naga, he used the power of this bow to shoot holes in the ships of her navy. This feat must have impressed the princess, because later she and Kaundinya were married. (*Liáng Shū.*)

Conqueror of the Three Worlds
COMES FROM: near Tibet
OWNED BY: Gesar of Ling

A mighty spear, decked all around with turquoise stones. Gesar acquired the Conqueror of the Three Worlds from a dungeon hidden within a crystal boulder in the forbidden kingdom of Jigdag Magyalpumra deep within the Himalayas. Among the number of ferocious monsters he had to face on the way was a so-called Cemetery Boar, which is presumably *more dangerous than a regular boar*, so you can see how difficult the task must have been. The spear's name may be a slight exaggeration. (*Epic of King Gesar.*)

Crooked Bow
COMES FROM: Iroquois Confederacy
OWNED BY: Bear Paw

Although this bow looks crooked and gnarled, arrows fired from it always fly true and hit their mark. Good for getting your opponent to underestimate your archery, possibly as part of a grift. (Iroquois legend.)

Dainsleif
COMES FROM: Denmark
OWNED BY: Hogni

The magical sword Dainsleif is guaranteed to kill someone every time it is drawn, and no wound it delivers, even a scratch, ever heals. In this way it is much like Tyrfing, except less cursed — although since Dainsleif's wielder, Hogni, must fight with it day after day, daily dying and daily resurrected in an eternal combat until doomsday . . . well, maybe that sounds like a curse as well. (*Skáldskaparmál.*)

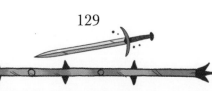

Excalibur's Scabbard
COMES FROM: Britain
OWNED BY: King Arthur

Excalibur is a great sword and all, but, as Merlin put it, "the scabbard is worth ten of the swords, for whiles ye have the scabbard upon you, ye shall never lose no blood, be ye never so sore wounded." Unfortunately, Arthur's sister Morgan le Fay stole the scabbard and replaced it with an ersatz duplicate. (*Le Morte d'Arthur.*)

Leg-biter
COMES FROM: Norway
OWNED BY: Gerimund the Noisy

Leg-biter is a beautiful sword, with a handle made from walrus ivory, but it is also cursed. Gerimund himself cursed it, when his wife Thurid stole it from him, calling upon the sword to draw Thurid's family's blood; soon her brother Kjartan and cousin Bolli were dead. Maybe that was the end of the curse, because other people have carried the sword without killing any of Thurid's relatives. A century later King Magnus Barefoot of Norway was wielding the sword when he was hacked to death with an ax, but that wasn't the sword's fault. Back then, Norwegian kings were always getting hacked to death, and it was just normal. (*Laxdæla Saga.*)

Lúin
COMES FROM: Ireland
OWNED BY: Celtchar mac Uthechar (but Mac Cécht borrowed it)

This gigantic spear kills nine men every time it is thrown. When used in battle it heats up until it bursts into flame, which can only be extinguished by dipping its head in a poisonous mixture of the blood of dogs and cats. (*Bruiðne Dá Derga.*)

Mech-samosek
COMES FROM: Russia
OWNED BY: Ivan the Guard

The self-swinging sword Mech-samosek was once owned by the nature-spirits of the Russian steppe, but when two of them quarreled over who should inherit the weapon, a passing guardsman named Ivan, under pretense of judging their quarrel, ran off with it. He used its power of flying from its wielder's hand and decapitating every being it comes across to work his way up from guardsman to prince. (Russian folklore.)

Nagastra
COMES FROM: Sri Lanka
OWNED BY: Indrajit

When fired from a bow, the magic snake-arrow Nagastra turns into thousands of poisonous snakes, possibly fire-breathing, that can either bind some victims like a thousand scaly ropes, or you know, kill them with poison and fire. Can be countered very specifically by the Garudastra, which chops off a thousand snakes' heads when fired. (*Ramayana.*)

Œgishjalmr, the Helm of Terror
COMES FROM: Scandinavia
OWNED BY: Sigurd

The Helm of Terror terrifies (of course) everyone who sees it. Sigurd plundered it from the hoard of the dragon Fafnir, and went around with this helmet on his head, just scaring everybody who looked at him. If Sigurd ever got some kind of device that made him invisible, that would probably ruin the whole power of the helm, so watch out for that. (*Volsunga Saga.*)

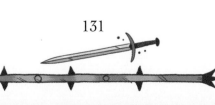

Shield of the Lion
COMES FROM: Germany
OWNED BY: Gasozein de Dragoz

In the center of this shield is mounted a lion's head with an open mouth, cunningly wrought so that wind whistling through the open mouth makes a moaning sound, somewhere between a lion's roar and a human voice. Also, the lion's tongue is on a hinge and can wiggle, which is a nice touch. Of course, if Gasozein had invested in a shield that did not have a hole in the middle, he may not have been defeated by Sir Gawain. (*Diu Crône.*)

Silken Green Girdle
COMES FROM: Britains
OWNED BY: Madame de Hautdesert

The most dangerous kind of magic item is one that *does not work*. The lady of Hautdesert loaned this girdle to Sir Gawain, promising it would protect him from all harm, including, most relevantly, being decapitated by her husband. The whole thing turned out to be a ruse. Fortunately for everyone, Mr. de Hautdesert was an understanding guy, and at decapitation time merely nicked Gawain's neck, but *thanks for nothing, girdle*! (*Sir Gawain and the Green Knight.*)

Sword of Mars
COMES FROM: Eurasian Steppes
OWNED BY: Attila the Hun

A Hunnic cowherd one day found one of his cows bleeding from a wound in the foot, and traced the trail of blood back to an ancient iron scimitar, barely sticking out of the ground. The cowherd dug up the scimitar and gave it to his king, Attila, who decided the sword gave him "divine and indefeasible claim to the dominion of the earth." At the very least, the sword let him conquer Europe, so partial credit. (Edward Gibbon.)

Tarnkappe
COMES FROM: Germany
OWNED BY: Sigurd

This cloak was long the patrimony of dwarven kings, such as King
Laurin (enemy of Dietrich of Bern), at least until Sigurd (who
was called Sigfried in Germany) wrested it from the dwarven king
Alberich (who was called Alfrik in Scandinavia). Not only does the
Tarnkappe render its wearer invisible, it gives them the strength of
twelve men or $1\frac{1}{5}$ Sir Galahads. (*Nibelungenlied*, et al.)

Twin Daggers of Nagurashkho son of Tlepsh
COMES FROM: Circassia
OWNED BY: Setenaya

When unsheathed, these daggers turn into a young man and woman
who will serve whoever drew them. They're good cooks, too! So
beautiful are the daggers, though, that whoever sees them will do
absolutely anything to acquire them, which you will perceive can
cause problems. (Nart sagas.)

Wolfskin Gloves
COMES FROM: Norway
OWNED BY: Queen Hvit

Anyone slapped by these gloves turns into a bear—inexplicably not
a wolf—forever. Queen Hvit used them against the warrior Bjorn,
who although a bear eventually fathered a human child, Bödvar . . .
who in turn killed Hvit in revenge. There's your boomerang! (*Hrólfs
Saga Kraka.*)

Egyptian

Norse

Persian

Arabian

Appendix B: Roll Call

Greek

European

Russian

Ethiopian

Aadi Madi-Karib
BORN: 6th-century Arabia
APPEARS IN: *Hamzanama*
HOUSE: Biscione
FOUND ON: 48

Achilles
BORN: 10th-century BC Greece
APPEARS IN: Greek myth
HOUSE: Biscione
FOUND ON: 26–27, 56, 81, 87

Aeneas
BORN: 10th-century BC Troy
APPEARS IN: *Aeneid*
HOUSE: Martlet
FOUND ON: 106

Ahaiyuta
BORN: 13th century in what is now New Mexico
APPEARS IN: Zuñi legend
HOUSE: Biscione
FOUND ON: 62

Aífe
BORN: 1st-century BC Scotland
APPEARS IN: The Ulster Cycle
HOUSE: Escallop
FOUND ON: 18–19

Alexander the Great
BORN: 4th-century BC Macedon
APPEARS IN: The Alexander romance
HOUSE: Biscione
FOUND ON: 11, 35, 72, 92

Alyosha Popovich
BORN: 10th-century Kiev
APPEARS IN: Russian legend
HOUSE: Martlet
FOUND ON: 29, 100

Amir Arsalan
BORN: 15th-century Egypt
APPEARS IN: *Amir Arsalan*
HOUSE: Martlet
FOUND ON: 59–60, 76

Amir Hamza
BORN: 6th-century Arabia
APPEARS IN: *Hamzanama*
HOUSE: Martlet
FOUND ON: 48

Amleth
BORN: 9th-century Denmark
APPEARS IN: *Gesta Danorum*
HOUSE: Pismire (long may it thrive!)
FOUND ON: 67, 84–86

"You know but little of the world . . . since you are
ignorant of what commonly occurs in knight-errantry."

–Cervantes, *Don Quixote* (1605)

Amphiaraus
BORN: 11th-century BC Greece
APPEARS IN: Greek myth
HOUSE: Martlet
FOUND ON: 56, 88–89

Ancaeus
BORN: 11th-century BC Samos
APPEARS IN: Greek myth
HOUSE: Biscione
FOUND ON: 55

Angantyr
BORN: 9th-century Norway
APPEARS IN: Norse sagas
HOUSE: Biscione
FOUND ON: 25, 78–79

Arjuna
BORN: 11th-century BC India
APPEARS IN: *Mahabharata*
HOUSE: Martlet
FOUND ON: 112

Arrow-Odd
BORN: 9th-century Norway
APPEARS IN: *Örvar-Odds Saga*
HOUSE: Biscione
FOUND ON: 44, 102

Arthur Pendragon
BORN: 5th-century Britain
APPEARS IN: Arthurian legend
HOUSE: Martlet
FOUND ON: 2

Aslak Holmskalli
BORN: 10th-century Denmark
APPEARS IN: *Jómsvíkinga Saga*
HOUSE: Biscione
FOUND ON: 25

Atalanta
BORN: 11th-century BC Greece
APPEARS IN: Greek myth
HOUSE: Escallop
FOUND ON: 56

Atli the Short
BORN: 10th-century Norway
APPEARS IN: *Egils Saga*
HOUSE: Biscione
FOUND ON: 27–28

Attila
BORN: 4th-century Hunnic
    Empire
APPEARS IN: Actual history
HOUSE: Biscione
FOUND ON: 123–24, 132

Aumon
BORN: 8th-century Spain
APPEARS IN: Carolingian legend
HOUSE: Martlet
FOUND ON: 81–82, 122

Bahram Gur
BORN: 5th-century Persia
APPEARS IN: *Shahnameh*
HOUSE: Escallop (house
    captain)
FOUND ON: 38

Baldwin
BORN: 5th-century Britain
APPEARS IN: *The Avowing of
    Arthur*
HOUSE: Martlet
FOUND ON: 99, 118–19

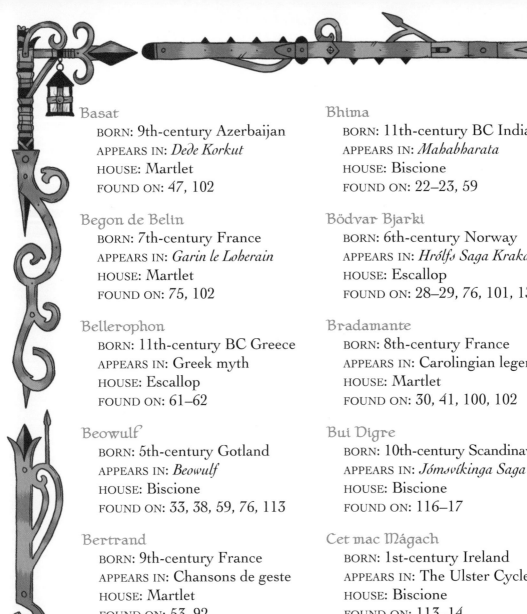

Basat
    BORN: 9th-century Azerbaijan
    APPEARS IN: *Dede Korkut*
    HOUSE: Martlet
    FOUND ON: 47, 102

Begon de Belin
    BORN: 7th-century France
    APPEARS IN: *Garin le Loherain*
    HOUSE: Martlet
    FOUND ON: 75, 102

Bellerophon
    BORN: 11th-century BC Greece
    APPEARS IN: Greek myth
    HOUSE: Escallop
    FOUND ON: 61–62

Beowulf
    BORN: 5th-century Gotland
    APPEARS IN: *Beowulf*
    HOUSE: Biscione
    FOUND ON: 33, 38, 59, 76, 113

Bertrand
    BORN: 9th-century France
    APPEARS IN: Chansons de geste
    HOUSE: Martlet
    FOUND ON: 53, 92

Bevis
    BORN: 10th-century
      Southampton, England
    APPEARS IN: Medieval legend
    HOUSE: Martlet
    FOUND ON: 56–57, 76, 92

Bhima
    BORN: 11th-century BC India
    APPEARS IN: *Mahabharata*
    HOUSE: Biscione
    FOUND ON: 22–23, 59

Bödvar Bjarki
    BORN: 6th-century Norway
    APPEARS IN: *Hrólfs Saga Kraka*
    HOUSE: Escallop
    FOUND ON: 28–29, 76, 101, 133

Bradamante
    BORN: 8th-century France
    APPEARS IN: Carolingian legend
    HOUSE: Martlet
    FOUND ON: 30, 41, 100, 102

Bui Digre
    BORN: 10th-century Scandinavia
    APPEARS IN: *Jómsvíkinga Saga*
    HOUSE: Biscione
    FOUND ON: 116–17

Cet mac Mágach
    BORN: 1st-century Ireland
    APPEARS IN: The Ulster Cycle
    HOUSE: Biscione
    FOUND ON: 113–14

Conall Cernach
    BORN: 1st-century Ireland
    APPEARS IN: The Ulster Cycle
    HOUSE: Martlet
    FOUND ON: 114

Conán mac Morna
    BORN: 4th-century Ireland
    APPEARS IN: The Fenian Cycle
    HOUSE: Pismire (tarantara!)
    FOUND ON: 18–19, 101

Cúchulainn
BORN: 1st-century Ireland
APPEARS IN: The Ulster Cycle
HOUSE: Biscione (house captain)
FOUND ON: 18–21, 25–27, 74, 76, 92, 120

Culhwch
BORN: 5th-century Wales
APPEARS IN: *Mabinogion*
HOUSE: Martlet
FOUND ON: 105, 108

David
BORN: 11th-century BC Israel
APPEARS IN: 1 & 2 Samuel
HOUSE: Martlet
FOUND ON: 46, 98

Diarmuid O'Duibhne
BORN: 4th-century Ireland
APPEARS IN: The Fenian Cycle
HOUSE: Escallop
FOUND ON: 57–58, 76, 101

Dietrich of Bern
BORN: 5th-century Roman empire
APPEARS IN: The Dietrich Cycle
HOUSE: Martlet
FOUND ON: 42, 71, 76, 86, 89–90

Digenes Akrites
BORN: 9th-century Anatolia
APPEARS IN: Greek folk epic
HOUSE: Escallop
FOUND ON: 63–64

Dinadan
BORN: 5th-century Britain
APPEARS IN: Arthurian legend
HOUSE: Pismire (glorious in memory!)
FOUND ON: 10–13, 16, 99

Queen of Easaidh Ruadh
BORN: 9th-century Scotland
APPEARS IN: Scottish legend
HOUSE: Unclear if she matriculated
FOUND ON: 44–45

Egil Skallagrimsson
BORN: 10th-century Iceland
APPEARS IN: *Egils Saga*
HOUSE: Biscione (double major)
FOUND ON: 27–28, 75

Enkidu
BORN: 65th-century BC Mesopotamia
APPEARS IN: *Gilgamesh*
HOUSE: Escallop
FOUND ON: VII, 102

Er Töshtük
BORN: 9th-century Kyrgyzstan
APPEARS IN: *The Epic of Manas*
HOUSE: Biscione
FOUND ON: 99, 106–7

Ferdiad
BORN: 1st-century Ireland
APPEARS IN: The Ulster Cycle
HOUSE: Biscione
FOUND ON: 26–27, 120

Finn Mac Cool
BORN: 4th-century Ireland
APPEARS IN: The Fenian Cycle
HOUSE: Escallop
FOUND ON: 40, 57–58, 101

Galahad
BORN: 6th-century Britain
APPEARS IN: Arthurian legend
HOUSE: Martlet
FOUND ON: 29, 87, 99, 105

Galien le Restoré
BORN: 9th-century France
APPEARS IN: Carolingian legend
HOUSE: Martlet
FOUND ON: 75

Gareth
BORN: 6th-century Scotland
APPEARS IN: Arthurian legend
HOUSE: Martlet
FOUND ON: 7, 9

Gasozein de Dragoz
BORN: 5th-century German
  states
APPEARS IN: *Diu Crône*
HOUSE: Biscione
FOUND ON: 111, 132

Gawain
BORN: 5th-century Scotland
APPEARS IN: Arthurian legend
HOUSE: Martlet
FOUND ON: 28, 76, 87, 92, 99,
  111, 132

St. George
BORN: 3rd-century Cappadocia,
  Asia Minor
APPEARS IN: Medieval legend
HOUSE: Martlet
FOUND ON: 37

Gesar of Ling
BORN: 10th-century Tibet
APPEARS IN: Tibetan and
  Mongolian legend
HOUSE: Martlet
FOUND ON: 59, 129

Gilgamesh
BORN: 65th-century BC Uruk
APPEARS IN: *Gilgamesh*
HOUSE: Biscione
FOUND ON: 102

Grettir the Strong
BORN: 10th-century Iceland
APPEARS IN: *Grettla*
HOUSE: Biscione
FOUND ON: 25

Guillaume d'Orange
BORN: 9th-century France
APPEARS IN: Chansons de geste
HOUSE: Martlet
FOUND ON: 13–15, 53–54, 75,
  92, 121

Gunther
BORN: 5th-century Burgundy
APPEARS IN: *Nibelungenlied*
HOUSE: Martlet
FOUND ON: 124

Hagen
BORN: 5th-century Burgundy
APPEARS IN: *Nibelungenlied*
HOUSE: Biscione
FOUND ON: 124

Hans Talhoffer
BORN: 15th-century Swabia
APPEARS IN: *Fechtbuch*
HOUSE: Martlet
FOUND ON: 86

Harishikha
BORN: 10th-century India
APPEARS IN:
Brihatkathaslokasangraha
HOUSE: Martlet
FOUND ON: 23

Hector
BORN: 10th-century BC Troy
APPEARS IN: Greek myth
HOUSE: Martlet
FOUND ON: 81

Henry de Sainct Didier
BORN: 16th-century France
APPEARS IN: *Les secrets du premier livre sur l'espée seule*
HOUSE: Martlet
FOUND ON: 17

Hercules
BORN: 11th-century BC Greece
APPEARS IN: Greek myth
HOUSE: Biscione
FOUND ON: 42, 59, 74, 108–9

Hereward the Wake
BORN: 11th-century England
APPEARS IN: *Gesta Herewardi*
HOUSE: Escallop
FOUND ON: 17

Hervarth
BORN: 9th-century Norway
APPEARS IN: Norse sagas
HOUSE: Biscione
FOUND ON: 78

Hjalmar
BORN: 9th-century Sweden
APPEARS IN: Norse sagas
HOUSE: Martlet
FOUND ON: 78, 102, 110

Hjalti
BORN: 6th-century Denmark
APPEARS IN: *Hrólfs Saga Kraka*
HOUSE: Escallop
FOUND ON: 29, 101

Hrolf Kraki
BORN: 6th-century Denmark
APPEARS IN: *Hrólfs Saga Kraka*
HOUSE: Martlet
FOUND ON: 28, 83, 96, 101, 119

Iktomi
BORN: 13th-century Great Lakes region
APPEARS IN: Lakota myth
HOUSE: Pismire (those bright school days of yore!)
FOUND ON: 66, 71–72

Ilya Muromets
BORN: 10th-century Kiev
APPEARS IN: Russian legend
HOUSE: Martlet
FOUND ON: 4–5, 9, 50–51, 89, 100

Jack the Giant Killer
BORN: 6th-century Cornwall
APPEARS IN: British folklore
HOUSE: Pismire (a proud tear comes to my eye)
FOUND ON: 40, 51

Jason
BORN: 11th-century BC Greece
APPEARS IN: Greek myth
HOUSE: Biscione
FOUND ON: 4, 9, 56, 105

Kalevipoeg
BORN: 1st-century BC Estonia
APPEARS IN: *Kalevipoeg*
HOUSE: Biscione
FOUND ON: 79–80

Kara Tygan Khan
BORN: 16th-century Siberia
APPEARS IN: *Kara Tygan Khan and Suksagal Khan*
HOUSE: Biscione
FOUND ON: 114–15

Karna
BORN: 11th-century BC India
APPEARS IN: *Mahabharata*
HOUSE: Martlet
FOUND ON: 111–12

Kay
BORN: 5th-century Britain
APPEARS IN: Arthurian legend
HOUSE: Pismire (ah, blessed memories!)
FOUND ON: 7, 99

Kemp Owyne
BORN: 5th-century Scotland
APPEARS IN: Childe ballads
HOUSE: Martlet
FOUND ON: 36

Ken Angrok
BORN: 12th-century Java
APPEARS IN: *Pararaton*
HOUSE: Biscione
FOUND ON: 82–83

Kormak Ogmundsson
BORN: 10th-century Iceland
APPEARS IN: *Kormáks Saga*
HOUSE: Biscione
FOUND ON: 78, 84

Kuskun Kara Mattyr
BORN: 16th-century Siberia
APPEARS IN: *Kogutei: Altaiski Epos*
HOUSE: Martlet
FOUND ON: 94–95

Lamorak
BORN: 5th-century Britain
APPEARS IN: Arthurian legend
HOUSE: Martlet
FOUND ON: 11–13, 99

Lancelot
BORN: 5th-century Brittany
APPEARS IN: Arthurian legend
HOUSE: Martlet (house captain)
FOUND ON: 7, 11, 38, 47, 69–70, 76, 99

Lemminkäinen
BORN: 1st-century BC Finland
APPEARS IN: The *Kalevala*
HOUSE: Biscione
FOUND ON: 105

Mac Cécht
BORN: 1st-century Ireland
APPEARS IN: The Ulster Cycle
HOUSE: Escallop
FOUND ON: 49–50, 130

Meleager
BORN: 11th-century BC Greece
APPEARS IN: Greek myth
HOUSE: Escallop
FOUND ON: 56

Menelaus
BORN: 10th-century BC Greece
APPEARS IN: Greek myth
HOUSE: Martlet
FOUND ON: 60

Menestratos
BORN: 12th-century BC Thespiae
APPEARS IN: *Hellados Periegesis*
HOUSE: Martlet
FOUND ON: 38

Michel Ney
BORN: 18th-century French borderlands
APPEARS IN: Actual history
HOUSE: Biscione
FOUND ON: 121

Miyamoto Musashi
BORN: 16th-century Japan
APPEARS IN: Actual history
HOUSE: Martlet
FOUND ON: 7, 16–17, 23, 76

Mwindo
BORN: 9th-century Zaire
APPEARS IN: Nyanga legend
HOUSE: Escallop
FOUND ON: 104–5

Odysseus
BORN: 10th-century BC Ithaca
APPEARS IN: Greek myth
HOUSE: Pismire (house captain)
FOUND ON: 47, 65, 105

Ogier the Dane
BORN: 8th-century Denmark
APPEARS IN: Carolingian legend
HOUSE: Biscione
FOUND ON: 76, 92, 100, 120–21

Oishi Kuranosuke
BORN: 17th-century Japan
APPEARS IN: *Chuushingura*
HOUSE: Martlet
FOUND ON: 72–73

Olaf Tryggvason
BORN: 10th-century Norway
APPEARS IN: *Óláfs Saga Tryggvasonar*
HOUSE: Biscione
FOUND ON: 16

Oliver
BORN: 8th-century France
APPEARS IN: Carolingian legend
HOUSE: Martlet
FOUND ON: 75–76, 100, 102, 122–23

Orfeo
BORN: 4th-century Winchester, Britain
APPEARS IN: *Sir Orfeo*
HOUSE: Martlet
FOUND ON: 105, 110

Orson
BORN: 8th-century France
APPEARS IN: *Valentin et Orson*
HOUSE: Escallop
FOUND ON: 102–3

Ortnit
BORN: 10th-century Lombardy
APPEARS IN: *Ortnit*
HOUSE: Martlet
FOUND ON: 76, 89, 95

Osla Gyllellfawr
BORN: 5th-century Wales
APPEARS IN: *Mabinogion*
HOUSE: Biscione
FOUND ON: 64–65

Sir Palamedes
BORN: 5th-century Palestine
APPEARS IN: Arthurian legend
HOUSE: Martlet
FOUND ON: 99, 104–5

King Pellinore
BORN: 5th-century in "the Isles" off Britain
APPEARS IN: Arthurian legend
HOUSE: Martlet
FOUND ON: 99, 104

Penthesilea
BORN: 10th-century BC Themiscyra
APPEARS IN: Greek myth
HOUSE: Escallop
FOUND ON: 81

Perceval
BORN: 6th-century Wales
APPEARS IN: Arthurian legend
HOUSE: Martlet
FOUND ON: VIII–IX, 99, 105

Peter Loschy
BORN: 14th-century England
APPEARS IN: Yorkshire folklore
HOUSE: Martlet
FOUND ON: 32–33, 38

Peucestas
BORN: 4th-century BC Macedon
APPEARS IN: Actual history
HOUSE: Martlet
FOUND ON: 3

Pinabel
BORN: 9th-century France
APPEARS IN: *La Chanson de Roland*
HOUSE: Biscione
FOUND ON: 71

Pirithous
BORN: 11th-century BC Greece
APPEARS IN: Greek myth
HOUSE: Biscione
FOUND ON: 56, 108–9

Ragnar Loth-brok
BORN: 8th-century Sweden
APPEARS IN: Norse sagas
HOUSE: Biscione
FOUND ON: 33

Rainouart
BORN: 9th-century Spain
APPEARS IN: Chansons de geste
HOUSE: Biscione
FOUND ON: 53–54

Raoul de Cambrai
BORN: 10th-century France
APPEARS IN: Chansons de geste
HOUSE: Biscione
FOUND ON: 71

Renaud de Montauban
BORN: 8th-century France
APPEARS IN: Carolingian legend
HOUSE: Martlet
FOUND ON: 75–76, 92–93, 100, 123

Richard Witherington
BORN: 14th-century Northumberland, England
APPEARS IN: *The Ballad of Chevy Chase*
HOUSE: Escallop
FOUND ON: 120

Robin Hood
BORN: 12th-century Huntingdon, England
APPEARS IN: English ballads
HOUSE: Escallop
FOUND ON: 66, 96–98

Roger
BORN: 8th-century Morocco
APPEARS IN: Carolingian legend
HOUSE: Martlet
FOUND ON: 76, 90, 100, 102

Roland
BORN: 8th-century France
APPEARS IN: Carolingian legend
HOUSE: Biscione
FOUND ON: 59, 71, 81–82, 92, 100, 102, 122–23

Rostam
BORN: 10th-century BC Persia
APPEARS IN: The *Shahnameh*
HOUSE: Biscione
FOUND ON: 37, 74, 90–91, 128

Saljan
BORN: 9th-century Trebizond
APPEARS IN: *Dede Korkut*
HOUSE: Escallop
FOUND ON: 16

Salur Kazan
BORN: 9th-century Azerbaijan
APPEARS IN: *Dede Korkut*
HOUSE: Martlet
FOUND ON: 38

Sam
BORN: 11th-century BC Persia
APPEARS IN: The *Shahnameh*
HOUSE: Martlet
FOUND ON: ii, 35

Sayf Ben Dhi Yazan
BORN: 6th-century Ethiopia
APPEARS IN: *Sirat Sayf Ben Dhi Yazan*
HOUSE: Martlet
FOUND ON: 80–81, 102

Scáthach
BORN: 1st-century BC Scotland
APPEARS IN: The Ulster Cycle
HOUSE: Escallop
FOUND ON: 18–19

Sesostris
BORN: 19th-century BC Egypt
APPEARS IN: Herodotus
HOUSE: Biscione
FOUND ON: 70

Shapur Z'ul Aktaf
BORN: 4th-century Persia
APPEARS IN: The *Shahnameh*
HOUSE: Martlet
FOUND ON: 68

Sigmund
BORN: 5th-century Scandinavia
APPEARS IN: *Völsunga Saga*
HOUSE: Biscione
FOUND ON: 33, 68–69

Sigurd the Dragon Slayer
BORN: 5th-century Scandinavia
APPEARS IN: *Völsunga Saga*
HOUSE: Biscione
FOUND ON: 26–27, 33–34, 92, 131, 133

Sigurd Fairhair
BORN: 10th-century Scandinavia
APPEARS IN: *Jómsvíkinga Saga*
HOUSE: Biscione
FOUND ON: 116–17, 125

Sigvaldi Strut-Haraldsson
BORN: 10th-century Scandinavia
APPEARS IN: *Jómsvíkinga Saga*
HOUSE: Biscione
FOUND ON: 115–17

Skarphedinn Njalsson
BORN: 10th-century Iceland
APPEARS IN: *Njála*
HOUSE: Martlet
FOUND ON: 22, 70

Starkad
BORN: 3rd-century Sweden
APPEARS IN: *Gesta Danorum*
HOUSE: Escallop
FOUND ON: 121–22

Svafrlami
BORN: 3rd-century Sweden
APPEARS IN: Norse sagas
HOUSE: Biscione
FOUND ON: 77–78

Svyatogor
BORN: 10th-century Kiev
APPEARS IN: Russian legend
HOUSE: Biscione
FOUND ON: 50–51, 100

Theseus
BORN: 11th-century BC Greece
APPEARS IN: Greek myth
HOUSE: Martlet
FOUND ON: 56, 59, 108–9

Thierry
BORN: 9th-century France
APPEARS IN: *La Chanson de Roland*
HOUSE: Martlet
FOUND ON: 71, 100

Thomas Hickathrift
BORN: 10th-century England
APPEARS IN: English folklore
HOUSE: Biscione
FOUND ON: 46

Thorkill the High
BORN: 10th-century Denmark
APPEARS IN: *Jómsvíkinga Saga*
HOUSE: Biscione
FOUND ON: 116–17, 125–26

Tom Thumb
BORN: 6th-century Britain
APPEARS IN: English chapbooks
HOUSE: Martlet
FOUND ON: 46–47, 99

Tristram
BORN: 5th-century Cornwall
APPEARS IN: Arthurian legend
HOUSE: Martlet
FOUND ON: 37, 46

Vagn Akason
BORN: 10th-century Denmark
APPEARS IN: *Jómsvíkinga Saga*
HOUSE: Biscione
FOUND ON: 115–16, 125

Valentine
BORN: 8th-century France
APPEARS IN: *Valentin et Orson*
HOUSE: Martlet
FOUND ON: 102–3

Vigfus Vigaglumsson
BORN: 10th-century Norway
APPEARS IN: *Jómsvíkinga Saga*
HOUSE: Biscione
FOUND ON: 25

Vivien
BORN: 9th-century France
APPEARS IN: Chansons de geste
HOUSE: Martlet
FOUND ON: 15

Warzameg
BORN: 8th-century Circassia
APPEARS IN: Nart sagas
HOUSE: Biscione
FOUND ON: 46, 104

Witege
BORN: 5th-century Denmark
APPEARS IN: The Dietrich Cycle
HOUSE: Biscione
FOUND ON: 86, 92

Yamato Takeru
BORN: 2nd-century Japan
APPEARS IN: Japanese legend
HOUSE: Biscione
FOUND ON: 64, 85–86

Yvain
BORN: 5th-century Britain
APPEARS IN: Arthurian legend
HOUSE: Escallop
FOUND ON: 93–94, 99

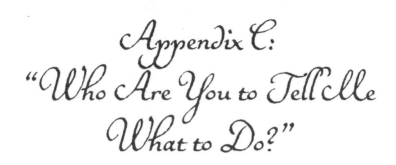

Appendix C: "Who Are You to Tell Me What to Do?"

That's what you should say to these people, and their books:

Aeschylus. *Seven Against Thebes*.
Ludovico Ariosto. *Orlando Furioso*.
Martha Warren Beckwith. *Mythology of the Oglala Dakota*.
Constance Brittain Bouchard, ed. *Knights in History and Legend*.
Katharine M. Briggs. *The Fairies in English Tradition and Literature*.
Budha-svamin. *The Emperor of the Sorcerers*.
John Francis Campbell, ed. *Popular Tales of the West Highlands*.
Richard Cavendish, ed. *Legends of the World*.
Nora Kershaw Chadwick. *Stories and Ballads of the Far Past*.
Nora Kershaw Chadwick and Victor Zhirmunsky. *Oral Epics of Central Asia*.
Chrétien de Troyes. *Romances*.
John Colarusso. *Nart Sagas*.
W. G. Collingwood and Jón Stefánsson, trans. *The Life and Death of Cormac the Skald*.
Nirmal Dass, trans. *The Avowing of King Arthur*.
Alexandra David-Néel and Albert A. Yongden, trans. *The Superhuman Life of Gesar of Ling*.
Paul B. Du Chaillu. *The Viking Age*.
Egil's Saga.
A. Ferdowsi. *Shahnameh*.
Joan M. Ferrante, trans. *Guillaume D'Orange: Four Twelfth-Century Epics*.
Nizami Ganjavi. *The Sikandar Nama,e Bara, or Book of Alexander the Great*.
Jeffrey Gantz. *Early Irish Myths and Sagas*.
George Laurence Gomme, ed. *The History of Thomas Hickathrift*.
Robert Graves. *The Greek Myths*.
Edward R. Haymes, trans. *Saga of Thidrek of Bern*.
Ronald B. Herzman, et al., eds. *Four Romances of England*.

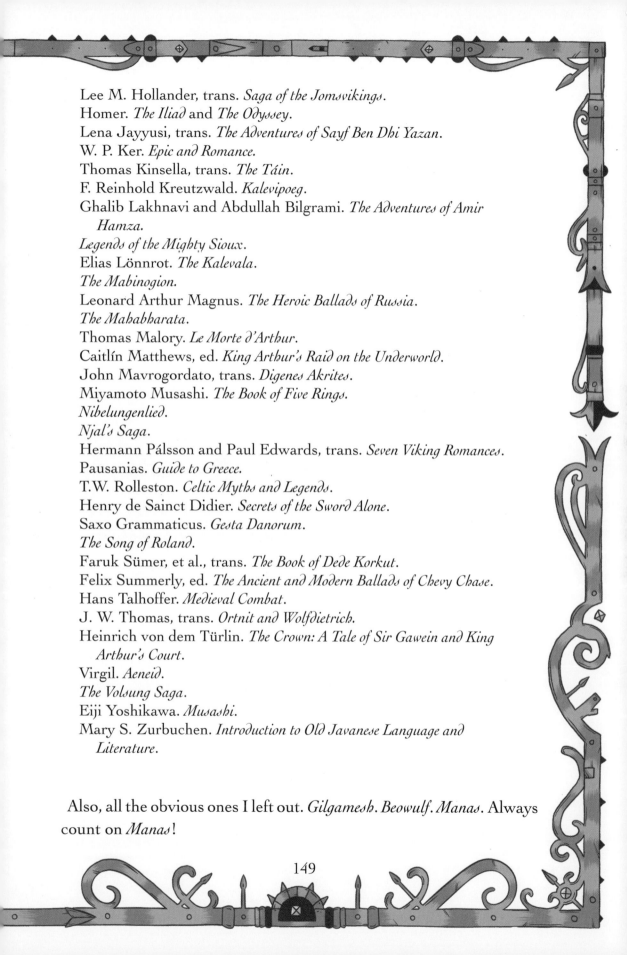

Lee M. Hollander, trans. *Saga of the Jomsvikings*.

Homer. *The Iliad* and *The Odyssey*.

Lena Jayyusi, trans. *The Adventures of Sayf Ben Dhi Yazan*.

W. P. Ker. *Epic and Romance*.

Thomas Kinsella, trans. *The Táin*.

F. Reinhold Kreutzwald. *Kalevipoeg*.

Ghalib Lakhnavi and Abdullah Bilgrami. *The Adventures of Amir Hamza*.

Legends of the Mighty Sioux.

Elias Lönnrot. *The Kalevala*.

The Mabinogion.

Leonard Arthur Magnus. *The Heroic Ballads of Russia*.

The Mahabharata.

Thomas Malory. *Le Morte d'Arthur*.

Caitlín Matthews, ed. *King Arthur's Raid on the Underworld*.

John Mavrogordato, trans. *Digenes Akrites*.

Miyamoto Musashi. *The Book of Five Rings*.

Nibelungenlied.

Njal's Saga.

Hermann Pálsson and Paul Edwards, trans. *Seven Viking Romances*.

Pausanias. *Guide to Greece*.

T.W. Rolleston. *Celtic Myths and Legends*.

Henry de Sainct Didier. *Secrets of the Sword Alone*.

Saxo Grammaticus. *Gesta Danorum*.

The Song of Roland.

Faruk Sümer, et al., trans. *The Book of Dede Korkut*.

Felix Summerly, ed. *The Ancient and Modern Ballads of Chevy Chase*.

Hans Talhoffer. *Medieval Combat*.

J. W. Thomas, trans. *Ortnit and Wolfdietrich*.

Heinrich von dem Türlin. *The Crown: A Tale of Sir Gawein and King Arthur's Court*.

Virgil. *Aeneid*.

The Volsung Saga.

Eiji Yoshikawa. *Musashi*.

Mary S. Zurbuchen. *Introduction to Old Javanese Language and Literature*.

Also, all the obvious ones I left out. *Gilgamesh. Beowulf. Manas*. Always count on *Manas*!

Hal Johnson is the author of several other books, including *Impossible Histories* and *Apprentice Academy: Sorcerers*. He has two kids, one wife, no tail, and eight-hundred thousand books (approx).

Cathrin Peterslund is an illustrator from Denmark. She graduated with a BA in graphic storytelling from The Animation Workshop in 2017. Since then, she has been working freelance in illustration, focusing on children's books and young fiction. She lives and works in Copenhagen, Denmark.

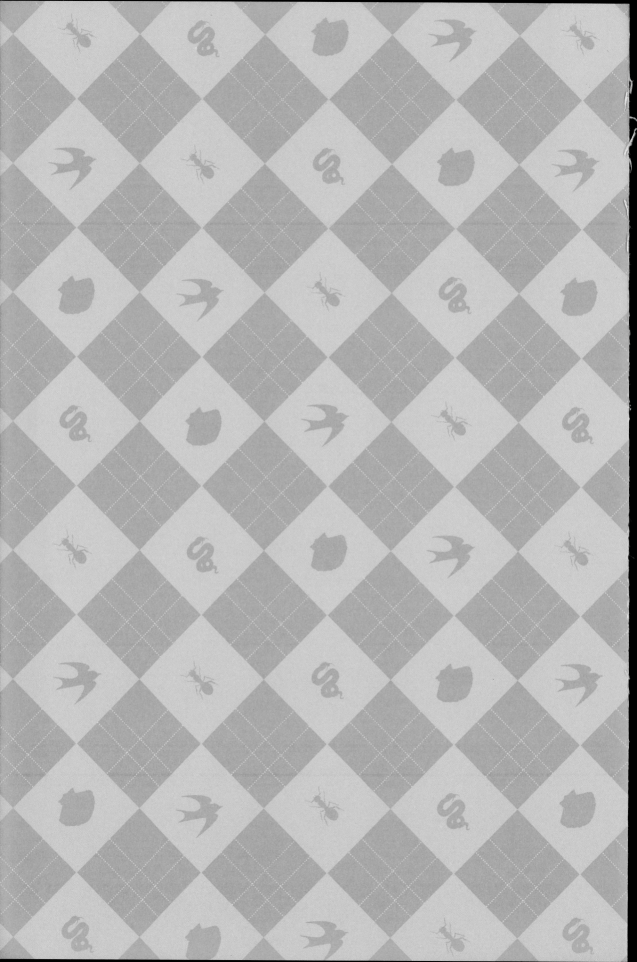